CHAKRA MANTRAS

(5 books In 1)

Meditation for beginners, Stress Management for beginners, Mindfulness Meditation, Increase Awareness and Expand Mind Power

Sarah Rowland

Copyright © 2017 by Sarah Rowland

All rights reserved. No part of this book may be reproduced or transmitted in any form or by any means, electronic or mechanical, including photocopying, recording or by any information storage and retrieval system without written permission of the publisher, except for the inclusion of brief quotations in a review.

TABLE OF CONTENTS

MEDITATION FOR BEGINNERS
Ultimate Guide To Relieve Stress, Depression And Anxiety

INTRODUCTION 2

Chapter 1 *The Basics*..4

Chapter 2 *Practice* 34

Chapter 3 *Common Pitfalls*..47

Chapter 4 *Keys To Success*... 60

Chapter 5 *Answers to Common Questions*.......................................76

Conclusion 84

Description 85

MINDFULNESS FOR BEGINNERS
Ultimate Guide To Achieve Happiness by Eliminating Stress, Depression and Anxiety

INTRODUCTION 87

Chapter 1 *The Power Of Mindfulness* 89

Chapter 2 *Simple Practices* 98

Chapter 3 *Advanced Practices* 114

Chapter 4 *Digging Deeper* 144

Conclusion 165

STRESS MANAGEMENT FOR BEGINNERS
Guided Meditation Techniques to Reduce Stress, Increase Happiness, and Improve your Health, Body & Mind

INTRODUCTION 169

Chapter 1 *What Is Stress?* 170

Chapter 2 *Process Stress In A Healthy Way – Eliminate Unnecessary Sources Of Stress* 176

Chapter 3 *Manage Stress With Food* 182

Chapter 4 *Manage Stress with Exercise* 189

Chapter 5 *Manage Stress With Sleep* 196

Chapter 6 *Manage Stress With Meditation* 202

Chapter 7 *Guided 5-Minute Meditation Session* 212

Chapter 8 *Guided 20 Minute Meditations Ession* 215

Chapter 9 *Manage Stress With Deep Breathing Exercises* 220

Chapter 10 *Maintain Activities With Positive People* 222

Chapter 11 *Daily Affirmations* 229

Chapter 12 *Positive Imagery* 235

Chapter 13 *Aromatherapy* 238

Conclusion 242

MINDFULNESS MEDITATION FOR SELF-HEALING

Beginner's Meditation Guide to Eliminate Stress and Anxiety, and Find Inner Peace and Happiness

INTRODUCTION 244

Chapter 1 *Understanding Mindfulness Meditation* 246

Chapter 2 *Mindfulness Meditation Basics* 252

Chapter 3 *Mindfulness During Your Commute* 263

Chapter 4 *Mindfulness On The Bus Or Train* 276

Chapter 5 *Mindfulness At Work* 282

Chapter 6 *Mindfulness At Home* 291

Chapter 8 *Tips For Improving Your Ability To Be Mindful* 309

Conclusion 317

YOU'RE ALL YOU NEED
Real Happiness Through The Power of Meditation

INTRODUCTION 320

Chapter 1 *What Is Meditation?* 321

Chapter 2 *43 Spectacular Benefits Of Meditation* 327

Chapter 3 *Types Of Meditation – Pick The One That Works For You.* 333

Chapter 4 *The 5-Minute Meditation* 342

Chapter 5 *10 Minute Guided Meditation Techniques* 345

Chapter 6 *The Fifteen Minute Anxiety Killing And Confidence Building Guided Meditation* 360

Chapter 7 *The Twenty Minute Body Scan* 373

Chapter 8 *The 25 Minute Blissful Mind Meditation* 382

Chapter 9 *The 30 -Minute Meditation* 396

Conclusion 415

MEDITATION FOR BEGINNERS

Ultimate Guide To Relieve Stress, Depression And Anxiety

Sarah Rowland

INTRODUCTION

Congratulations on downloading this book and thank you for doing so.

The following chapters will teach you everything that you need to know about meditation so that you can easily and quickly relieve yourself of stress, anxiety, and depression.

Chapter 1 discusses the basics of meditation, such as what meditation is, the different chakras, mindfulness, as well as how to practice meditation, among others.

Chapter 2 deals with the actual practice of meditation. You will learn different kinds of meditation techniques, such as breathing meditation, mantra meditation, chakra meditation, and even a way to meet your spirit guide.

Chapter 3 talks about the common pitfalls that beginners often encounter. It is important for you to know them so that you can avoid making the same mistakes.

Chapter 4 reveals the keys to success so that you can get the best benefits from your meditation practice.

Chapter 5 gives the answers to common questions about meditation.

There are plenty of books on this subject on the market; thanks again for choosing this one! Every effort was made to ensure it is full of as much useful information as possible. Please enjoy!

CHAPTER 1
The Basics

The practice of meditation can be traced back to ancient times. It is a common practice in Buddhism, Hinduism, and in many other spiritual traditions. But, what is meditation? Some say that it is a prayer or some form of mysticism, while others say that it is an art of transforming the mind. All these definitions may be true. Meditation is not really something that you define. It is something that you practice on a regular basis, and the only way to discover its true meaning is to experience it on your own.

Today, meditation is seen as an effective way to feel better, to reduce stress and anxiety, or simply a way to get a better quality of sleep. However, it should be noted that meditation is more spiritual than physical.

Power and benefits of meditation

Meditation offers enormous benefits, from physical, mental, emotional and, of course, spiritual benefits. Today, in a world full of busy people, meditation is usually promoted as a way to relieve stress. Although relieving stress is one of the benefits of meditation, it should be noted that meditation is more spiritual than physical. It was also through years of meditation that Siddhartha Gautama Buddha achieved enlightenment.

Meditation is a powerful spiritual practice that can alter your state of mind and change your life. On a spiritual level, regular practice of meditation can make you feel calmer and improve your sleep. It can also reduce anxiety and depression. Meditation is also able to boost your immune system by suppressing the production of stress hormone. A study conducted at Harvard Medical School also revealed that regular practice of meditation can significantly lower blood pressure.

On a spiritual level, meditation is a key to enlightenment. It also strengthens the aura, energizes your chakras, and develops your psychic senses. Also, when you go deep into meditation, you can have magical and divine experiences.

How to practice meditation

The best way to practice meditation is simply to do it regularly. There are many meditation techniques that you can find online or when you read books on this subject. There is really no right or wrong way to meditate, as long as it works for you. You can try all the different meditation techniques that you can find and then stick to the one that works best.

Meditation is not something that you do sparingly. If you really want to experience the enormous benefits that it offers, then you should meditate regularly. This means that you should meditate every day, or as often as you can.

One session of meditation may last for a few minutes or up to an hour, even several hours, or even for more than a day. It is not how long you meditate that matters, but the quality of your meditation.

You should not worry about time when you meditate. When you meditate and enter deeper states of consciousness, you will lose track of time. Some moments, time may seem to fly so quickly, while other moments it might seem to move so slowly. Of course, if you are too concerned of the time, you can always set an alarm clock to signal the end of a meditation session. Just remember to use a sound that is not too high or too loud; otherwise, you might get a headache. When you go deep in meditation, even the slightest sound can be a distraction. Therefore, when you use an alarm, it is good to use a gentle or soothing music, and do not make it too loud.

Preparation

Before you start meditating, it is important for you to know the right position. There are different positions that you can use: You can meditate in a sitting or cross-legged position on the floor, or even while lying down. You can also meditate while sitting on a chair. When sitting on a chair, you should keep your spine straight and your feet flat on the floor. Having your spine straight will allow the energy in your body to flow smoothly. If sitting on a chair, having the soles of your feet flat on the floor will make you more connected to the earth and feel more grounded and centered.

If you sit on the floor to meditate, you can put a cushion or a towel under your legs or knees to help you feel more comfortable. Again, the important part is to keep your spine straight.

Whether or not you should close your eyes while meditating is a matter of personal preference. But, to minimize distraction and feel more relaxed, it is recommended that you close your eyes when meditating.

You should, of course, choose a time that you will not be distracted. Turn your phone off or switch it to silent mode prior to meditation. Also, avoid wearing tight clothing, so that you will not feel uncomfortable. To be more comfortable, it is also suggested that you remove your shoes.

Many of those who meditate regularly like to create a special place where they do their meditation practice. It does not have to be a big space. In fact, it can be as simple as having a meditation space in a small corner of your room. After all, you do not move to places when you meditate, except when you practice walking meditation.

The moment of *Now*

All meditation techniques teach that you should exist and be present in the *Now*. Unfortunately, many people these days are unconscious of what they are doing. Meditation teaches that you should be here now, live, and experience life as it is. It should be noted that experiencing being present in the moment of *Now* is not a strange idea. One way or another, you have experienced this already. This is the moment when it seems like everything has fallen into place, or during moments of extreme emotions. For example, in a game of basketball, this is the time when a player is said to be "on fire." This moment can also be how you felt when you had your first intimate kiss with your loved one, where every small movement or sound felt so meaningful.

Imagination

Imagination is a key to enter a higher state of consciousness. It will allow you to visit a realm that would otherwise be hidden from the reality that you usually know. Some meditation techniques, especially those that deal with pathworking, will ask you to imagine a scene. For example, imagine walking on the shore. When you do this, it is important that you keep an open mind. Allow the imagined scene to unfold. Now, you might be wondering, "Is it real?" The answer to this question is still under controversy. Some believe that since you only deal with imagined scenes or objects, then it could not be real. However, there are those who believe that even imagined things somehow have an existence of their own. After all, simply having something in your mind already proves the fact that it exists. Otherwise, it could not even exist in your mind. Regardless whether you want to believe them to be real or not, the effects that they do remain beneficial. So, just try the meditation techniques in this book, and see for yourself.

A committee of minds

When you meditate, you may notice that you seem to have different minds. This is due to the fact that you have diverse ideas, and there are different ways to satisfy each one of them. Such ideas may vary from your different notions of what happiness is, how to satisfy different kinds of pleasure, up to your definition of yourself. By practicing meditation, you can get to still your minds and make them be in harmony with one another.

On mindfulness

Meditation teaches one to be mindful. This means that you should be conscious and truly exist in the present moment. Unfortunately, many people are not conscious of being alive. Such "unconsciousness" explains why even after talking to someone, you cannot even tell what the person is wearing, or not noticing the color of the ceiling even when you have been in the room for more than an hour already. Many people get used to their daily routine that they become like robots. Meditation seeks to remedy this problem by teaching you to be conscious and experience the beauty of being truly alive, where every breath matters.

How to use meditation to find true happiness from within

Any meditation technique can lead you to find inner happiness. When you meditate, you get to be in touch with the divine energy, and you get to discover your own divinity. This is not hard to achieve. In fact, in the first few days that you begin meditating, you may already feel some sort of happiness that explodes from within. As you continue to meditate, this happiness grows, and you will be able to tap it even when not meditating. It simply becomes a part of you. The key to finding true happiness from within is simply to meditate regularly.

It is important to note that true happiness does not just come by meditating. To make happiness real, there must also be a change of heart. When you meditate for a longer time, you may notice that you become kinder and gentler, especially if you regularly work on your heart chakra. You should allow such positive changes to manifest themselves through your actions. You also cannot expect to have a peaceful and happy life if you are not at peace with yourself. By meditating, you get to still the mind and free your real self. Making peace with yourself is often the key to improving your relationship with other people. Simply put, the practice of meditation will give you a sense of peace and happiness, but if you want to make such development to be meaningful, then you should share such positive energies with everyone.

What is a mantra?

A mantra is a word, syllable, or sound, that functions as the point of focus in meditation. The most common mantra is the mantra *OM* or *AUM*. This mantra is usually practiced in Buddhism, Hinduism, as well as in other spiritual traditions. According to Pranic Healing Grandmaster Choa Kok Sui, the mantra *OM* was the very first sound in the universe.

There are different kinds of mantras. In fact, you can even make your own mantra. By having a mantra to focus on, you get to shut other thoughts from entering your mind. And, in case other thoughts are able to penetrate your mind, you can avoid clinging to these thoughts simply by shifting your focus back on your mantra. Again, your mantra is your point of focus in meditation. Remember: When you meditate, nothing should exist in your mind, except your mantra.

Meditation is a holy pilgrimage, and your mantra is the vehicle that you use to reach your destination. Therefore, it is important that you learn to be one with your mantra. Of course, the way to do this is to keep on chanting your mantra and meditating regularly.

Monkey mind

When you first start meditating, you may find that it is hard to control your thoughts. Many thoughts may arise as you meditate, such as what are you going to have for dinner, things that you need to do for work or school, some people that you need to talk to, or even if what you are doing actually makes any sense. In Buddhism, this is called as the *monkey mind*, where your mind jumps from one thought to another, just like a monkey jumping from one branch to another. Do not worry; this is normal. With consistent practice, you will be able to overcome this monkey mind. Remember that during meditation, you should be in the present moment called *Now*. Do not entertain other thoughts. After all, you can deal with your other concerns *after* meditation.

The chakras

The term *chakra* is a Sanskrit word which means *wheel*. The chakras are the energy centers in the body. The body, more specifically, your energy body, has seven major chakras located along the spine. On the one hand, when any of these chakras is not properly balanced, you may experience discomfort, serious stress, or even illness. On the other hand, if you have well-energized chakras, then you can enjoy a healthy body and a positive living. Having healthy chakras is also the way to a healthy body. It should be noted, however, that the physical body and the energy body are closely connected. If you want to have healthy chakras, you also need to take care of your physical body.

Crown chakra

The crown chakra is located just a little above your head. This chakra serves as the entry point for higher consciousness. This is the key to connecting with the higher self and cosmic consciousness. This chakra is strongly associated with divine intelligence and wisdom. Those with high spiritual realization have a more developed crown chakra. This is also what is symbolized by the crowns worn by kings and other royalties. The crown chakra is important in realizing the oneness of spirituality. It also affects your state of mind and how you think. When you develop your crown chakra, you should also work on your heart chakra. The color of this chakra is violet.

Ajna chakra

The ajna chakra, or more popularly known as the *third eye chakra*, is the seat of the intuition, which allows you to see psychic and spiritual visions. It is located between the eyebrows. If you want to develop psychic abilities such as clairvoyance, telepathy, remote viewing, and channeling, then this is the chakra that you should work on. The ajna chakra will allow you to see things as they truly are. When you first start to develop this chakra, the visions that you will get may not be as clear and correct as they should be. However, the visions will gradually improve, and you will get vivid and solid visions, and even see spirits in the astral dimension or the Otherworld. The color of this chakra is indigo.

Throat chakra

If you are having trouble with expressing yourself, then you should work on your throat chakra. Located in the throat, it is the realm of creative expression. It is about communication and voicing the truth. It should be noted that this chakra is not just about talking, but it also emphasizes the importance of listening. After all, every good communicator knows that listening is more important than talking. The color of this chakra is blue.

Heart chakra

The heart chakra is the center of universal love. It is located in the center of the chest at the level of the physical heart. If you are wondering why all the enlightened beings who walked the earth were so kind and loving, then the heart chakra explains it all. Although this chakra may be associated with romantic love shared between two people, the chakra is more about the universal type of love, such as love for your enemies, neighbors, and even for strangers. This chakra is an important part of any spiritual transformation. If you want to be more forgiving and kind, then you should work on your heart chakra. The color of this chakra is green.

Solar plexus chakra

The solar plexus chakra is associated with willpower. It is located in the solar plexus region. Since the meaningful things in life always require the exercise of willpower, this chakra is something that you cannot ignore. When you feel powerless and controlled by other people instead of being the master of your life, then it is usually a sign that you need to strengthen your solar plexus chakra. A common cause of an underdeveloped solar plexus chakra is when a child receives lots of discouragements instead of inspirations and motivations. The color of this chakra is yellow.

Sacral chakra

The sacral chakra, also known as *sex chakra* or *belly chakra,* is located about two inches below the navel. This chakra deals with sexuality and does not just refer to the mere act of lovemaking. It is also associated with expression through the sense of touch, such as an embrace. After all, procreation is only possible when there is an expression of strong emotions. If you have problems with your sexual life or in controlling your lust, or if you simply want to last longer in bed, then this chakra is something that you cannot ignore. The color of this chakra is orange.

Root chakra

This chakra is also known as the *base chakra*. It is located at the base of the spine and deals with security and safety. Located beneath the other main chakras, it also serves as a foundation. A strong base chakra will make you feel more grounded and stable. This chakra deals with the basic needs, such as a food and shelter. It also refers to your emotional and even spiritual needs. It is also the point for kundalini awakening. The color of this chakra is red.

Chakra colors

Knowing the colors of each chakra is essential so that you will know the right way to visualize the chakras during meditation. Although most meditation techniques do not require that you visualize any of the chakras, there are some techniques that will require you to *see* the chakras. By knowing their respective colors, you will be more able to connect with them.

Memorizing the colors of the seven chakras is very simple. As you may notice, they follow the colors of the rainbow: ROYGBIV. Where *R* or *Red* is the root chakra, and then up to *V* or *Violet* for the crown chakra.

What is the mind?

When you read about meditation, books on the subject always mention the word *mind*. But, what is this mind? Does it refer to your brain? It should be noted that mind in meditation does not only refer to your brain or your thoughts, but covers a more comprehensive meaning. In fact, it does not even refer to your mind. The mind is something that you do not see with your eyes. But, if the mind is not the brain or any other physical part that you can see, what can it be?

It should be understood that the mind and the body are two different things. For example, you can be very inactive in bed, but have wild and wonderful thoughts in your mind. The mind is formless. Some people figuratively call it the "heart." Like, when someone loves a person, he says that the person he loves is in his heart, yet he obviously does not refer to his physical heart. Now, it is important to control the mind, because happiness depends heavily on one's state of mind.

Levels of consciousness

When you meditate, you enter into different states of consciousness. The levels that you experience depend on how deep you are in meditation. There are seven states of consciousness, and they are the following:

The first three states are your normal waking consciousness, when you are in a deep sleep, and the state of dreaming. These three states are very much known to man, even to those who do not practice meditation. There are, however, three more states of consciousness that are rarely experienced.

The fourth state of consciousness is known as the transcendental consciousness. This is the state of total silence where the mind and all your senses are still; however, unlike sleeping, your consciousness remains awake so you are able to tell what is happening. Some meditators confuse this state with the devil's realm because you will experience a sense of bliss in this state. However, it should be noted that once you enter this state, you must keep on continuing your meditation, because there are other states to reach, and this should not be the end goal of meditation. But, if you only want to experience bliss and feel calmer, then this state of consciousness will not disappoint you.

The fifth level of consciousness is called cosmic consciousness. Here, you realize total detachment from the self and realize that you are nothing but consciousness. In this state, you will understand that you are not the body or the mind. You are only a consciousness. It is in this state where the ego totally disappears. And, by discovering what you are not, you get to realize who you truly are. This state of consciousness can be likened to the parable of the white room. The parable goes something like this: A man is in a white room all his life. One day, a ball enters the room, and he realizes that he is not the ball. The next day, an elephant enters, and he realizes that he is also not an elephant. The following day, an airplane enters the room, and he realizes that he is not an airplane, and so on and so forth. The more things that enter the room, the more he realizes who he is not; and by knowing who he is not, he gets to realize who he truly is. When you reach the fifth level of consciousness, the ego dissolves, the body and your sense of self get detached, and you realize that you are nothing but consciousness.

Again, this stage is not the end. Although what you can experience here would be mystifying, you must continue to meditate. If you use mantra meditation, then keep focusing on your mantra, for this is not the end of your spiritual pilgrimage.

The sixth level of consciousness is called God consciousness. Again, many meditators confuse this with the devil's realm. But, take note that this is not the final stage of meditation. When you reach this state, you will experience a feeling of great bliss. This is the state where you totally lose the self and find the Self, which is the divinity that lies within. It is during this state where you will feel your heart open up and experience a state of bliss that appears to be the purest of anything. If you are familiar with the Christian text that says that humans are made in the image and likeness of God, then this state of consciousness will make you feel, realize, and experience its true meaning. For, after all, there is divinity within each person. In this stage, you shall get in touch and experience that divinity, which is part of the divine essence of things.

The seventh level of consciousness, which is the highest state, is the unity consciousness. This is the stage of enlightenment and is the last stage of meditation. It may take you years to reach this stage. In Buddhism, this is the state of Nirvana, or eternal happiness. Here there is no more division between the inner and the outer, between the self and the Self, but everything reveals itself as one. This is the true realization of the oneness of spirituality. In this state, you experience and realize that the self and the Divine are one and the same, that you have always been part of the Divine energy. Indeed, here you will know that you are not simply made in the image and likeness of God, but that you have a god-self, where the divinity that lies within reveals itself completely.

Effects of stress, anxiety, and depression

The effects of stress, anxiety, depression, and all other negativity are harmful to your health and wellbeing. When you are in a state of negativity, the chakras weaken and blockages are made which prevent the smooth flow of energy. If left untreated, illness, disease, and other serious side effects can be expected to manifest in the physical body.

By practicing meditation, you can avoid the aforesaid side effects. It also does not matter which meditation technique you use, since all forms of meditation strengthen the aura, as well as your chakras and energy body.

You should understand that negative energies such as anxiety and stress are not good and that you always have a choice whether you want your life to be controlled by these negative forces or not. Let me repeat: You have a choice. If feeling stressed is something that you cannot control, just remember a saying in Buddhism: "If you can solve your problems, what is the use of worrying? If you cannot solve your problems, what is the use of worrying?" Therefore, do not worry. Worrying will only make you feel stressed out and create blockages.

Regardless what negative energy you are dealing with, meditation can help you feel so much better. But, just like any medicine, it may take time for you to actually feel the benefits of meditation. But, take note that no amount of meditation is ever wasted. You should meditate and persevere. If you do so, your perspective and mindset will change, and you can exercise mastery not just over you healthy, but also over yourself.

On happiness

Happiness is possible and is always within your reach regardless of your circumstances in life. Being happy is a state of mind, and it is a choice — a choice that only you can make. The good news is that meditation is a key to happiness. If you persist in this practice, you will soon discover a happiness that is impossible to describe, and this happiness can be eternal. Once you go deep in meditation and discover the mystery of a single breath or the beauty if a mantra, you will know that happiness has always been with you and that you only need to look within to find it.

Increase your vibration

Meditation is an effective way to increase your vibration. Your vibration is what controls your mental state. You draw certain energies or influences depending on your level of vibration. Negative and filthy things are associated with low vibrations, while pleasant things are associated with high vibrations. Now, you might be wondering, "How do I increase my vibration?" According to the Hermetic teachings, the way to increase your vibration can be done by using your will. You should use your will to focus on something that is positive and ignore negativity. Just simply focus and work on positive things. Take note that you do not deal directly with the negative stuff. This is because of the esoteric teaching that positive and negative are one and the same. They are only different in terms of degree. Also, even assuming that you removing a negative trait or quality, what then goes in its place? If nothing, then you will be left with emptiness even after removing a particular negativity. But, by working on positive energies, the negative qualities do not just disappear, but you also fill your life with happy, peaceful, and pleasant energies.

Remaining in a state of good vibration may be challenging. There are many things in life that can affect your mood and suddenly change your vibration. However, with persistence and continuous practice, you can maintain a state of high vibration for a longer period of time. Mastery of the self is the key.

What is the energy body?

As you read this book or any book in meditation, you will usually encounter the term *energy body*. Now, what is the energy body? Obviously, it does not refer to your physical body. Unless, if you want to consider your physical your body as a form of energy, which it is, then you may understand the term energy body to also refer to your physical body — which is fine. But, usually, the term energy body refers to that body that you have that is usually invisible to the naked eye. Taking care of your energy body is important because it strongly affects your physical body. In fact, a study shows that illnesses first manifest themselves in the energy body before they manifest in the physical body. This means that a healthy energy body translates to a healthy physical body. The good news is that the regular practices of meditation naturally strengthen your energy body. It is also worth noting that the energy body can be further classified into five layers:

The etheric body is that energy body that is just less than an inch away from your physical body. This is also the energy body that can easily be seen even by the naked eye under right circumstances. It is usually referred to as a blueprint of the physical body. After the etheric energy body, the next layer is called the emotional body or emotional energy body. As the name implies, this energy body acts as the storage of different emotions and feelings, such as your greatest joys and fears. This energy body usually changes depending on your current emotion or state of mind.

Right after the emotional body, there is the mental energy body. This energy body is composed of your so many ideas. Your thoughts arise and are stored in this energy body. This is also the reason why you should always think of happy and positive thoughts. If you keep on thinking negative thoughts, your mental energy body can be easily contaminated. Last but not least is the spiritual energy body. This energy body is usually associated with higher awareness.

It is worth noting that the different energy bodies, including your physical body, are interconnected. Each energy body can greatly affect the others. For example, when you always think positive thoughts, your mental energy body gets filled with positive energy, and since thoughts affect your emotions, even your emotional energy body gets affected. If any of your energy bodies carry positive energy, then it also reflects on your physical body. For example, by having an emotional energy body that is full of happy energy, your physical body also tends to reflect it by smiling or laughing. On a negative note, however, when your energy body is full of negativity, your physical body will also suffer. Therefore, it is important that you maintain a positive outlook and state of mind. The key to doing this is to learn to control your thoughts, and the best way to have mastery over your thoughts is by regular practice of meditation.

Signs of progress

Continuous practice is the key to progress in meditation. However, when you meditate on your row, it may be hard for you to measure or tell if you are getting any progress or not. Unfortunately, many people stop meditating because they think that they do not get any progress. It should be noted that no meditation practice is ever wasted, so do not think that you are not making any progress even if you do not notice any changes. Here are some signs that usually mean that you are progressing in your meditation practice:

More concentration – You may notice that your concentration has strengthened. This is a normal effect of any meditation technique. You will know that you develop more concentration when you can focus on your mantra (or any point of focus in meditation) without being distracted for a longer period.

Mystical experiences – Mystical experiences while meditating is also a common sign of progress. Do you see magical visions or feel an indescribable sense of bliss? This may also include simpler occurrences, such as having a rhythmic breathing, losing track of time, or seeing lights.

Posture is easily maintained – Pain or discomfort is common, especially when one has just started practicing meditation. However, as you progress in your meditation by your continuous practice, you may notice that your posture problems or discomfort suddenly disappear. Some people slouch when they meditate and feel uneasiness in their back to maintain the right posture. If you are one of these people but then suddenly notice that you have become used to the proper posture, then congratulate yourself for a nice progress.

Being more conscious during the waking state – Progress in meditation can also be seen not just during actual meditation, but also after meditation. Are you more conscious of yourself and the world during your normal state of consciousness? Those who progress in meditation tend to get more sensitive and become more appreciative of everything. In fact, even a flower or a sunset can become more beautiful than it used to be.

Time passes

As you go deeper into meditation, the more it would seem that time passes more quickly. If you find it easy to meditate for an hour without falling asleep, then it is a good sign that you are getting some progress.

Kindness

Since meditation develops the heart chakra, meditators also tend to be kind. If you notice yourself being kinder or nicer to everyone, then it may be another good sign of progress. After all, the true effects of meditation should be seen even when not meditating. Meditation should improve your character.

What other people say

Sometimes, it is what other people say that can make you realize any progress. It is not uncommon to be disappointed with a few failures that you miss out the good ones.

CHAPTER 2

Practice

Now that you have a basic knowledge of meditation, it is time for you to learn what meditation really is, and the only way to do this is by actual experience. The following will teach you various meditation techniques. Feel free to try each one of them. If getting enlightened is your goal, then it is suggested that you focus on mantra or breathing meditation. When you do any of these exercises, be sure to do so in a place where you will not be distracted. You also have to assume a proper asana or posture. As already mentioned in the previous chapter, you may meditate in a sitting position, or even while lying in bed. Should you choose to assume a lying down position, just remember that it may increase the chances of falling asleep. Regardless which position you use, the important thing is to keep your spine straight, so that the divine energy can flow smoothly and naturally.

You should also connect your tongue to your palate or the roof of your mouth. Such position improves the flow of energy and instantly strengthens the aura. You might find this uncomfortable in the beginning, but simply give yourself time to get used to it. In fact, as you get deeper in meditation, the tongue automatically connects itself to the palate.

Breathing meditation *(Duration: at least 5 minutes)*

Meditation on the breath is the simplest form of meditation. After all, what could be simpler than breathing? Although very simple, it is very effective. In fact, many meditators spend years by only practicing breathing meditation. This meditation technique has all the benefits that you can expect from meditation, such as relaxation, mental alertness, better quality of sleep, inner sense of peace and happiness, as well as spiritual awakening, among others.

1. Assume a proper position for meditation.
2. Close your eyes and relax.
3. Focus on your breathing. Your breathing is your mantra.
4. Should other thoughts arise, stay calm and relaxed, and gently focus back on your breathing.
5. Breathe in, and out.
6. Relax.

(Wait for at least five minutes)

7. Gently, bring your attention back to your physical body.
8. It is time to return to normal consciousness.
9. Slowly, open your eyes.

Mantra meditation *(Duration: at least 5 minutes)*

Mantra meditation is as common as breathing meditation, and it is very effective. Of course, the first step is for you to have a mantra. A recommended mantra to use is the mantra *OM*. When you say your mantra, you should pronounce it with a resonating sound.

If you want, you can also make your own mantra. Your mantra can be anything. It can be a word or even just a syllable. If you choose to use your own mantra, just remember that your mantra should not evoke images or emotions in your mind. Therefore, do not use the mantra *car* because it will compel you to imagine a car. Also, avoid using long mantras, so you will not have any problem with memorizing and pronouncing it over and over again.

1. Close your eyes.
2. Relax.

3. Chant your mantra.

4. Focus on your mantra.

5. Nothing should exist but your mantra.

6. Focus and be one with your mantra.

7. Let go of everything. Embrace your mantra.

8. Once you want to end the meditation session, just gently think of your body, and then slowly open your eyes.

Chakra meditation *(Duration: at least 25 minutes)*

This meditation will energize your chakras, cleanse negative energies, and remove any blockages. The steps are as follows:

Close your eyes. Relax. Inhale. As you exhale, imagine exhaling all the stress and tensions in your body. Take a slow, deep breath. Exhale. Imagine white light descending from heaven. It is a divine light, powerful, pure white, and radiant. See and feel it descend down to your crown chakra, charging it with energy. See your crown chakra and its violet color radiating stronger, and stronger. Keep charging your crown chakra. Remember that this ray of energy is pure, powerful, and infinite. See your crown chakra glowing, getting more powerful every second.

Now, let the ray of divine light descend more, and feel as it enters the top of your head. Feel its purity and invigorating energy. See and feel as it touches your third eye chakra. Your third eye chakra is the seat of intuition. See its indigo color shining brightly as it is being charged with the divine ray of energy. As your third eye chakra gets stronger and stronger, you know that you can see through everything. Nothing can be hidden from you, because your intuition and psychic vision can penetrate through everything. Keep on charging your third eye. Feel the immense power that you are receiving.

Slowly, the divine light descends down to the next chakra, your throat chakra. Let is energize your throat chakra. Imagine yourself being comfortable in a conversation, expressing your wonderful thoughts. See yourself and everyone else smiling. You are a good communicator. You have raw creative talents. Keep charging your throat chakra. Know that the more you charge it, the better you become.

See the white light flow down slowly into your heart chakra. Imagine yourself with your family and friends having a good time. Imagine soldiers shaking hands and embracing one another. See yourself doing good deeds to people. How does it feel to love and be loved, all the time? See and feel your heart chakra expanding and glowing, so bright it is blinding. After all the hate, now you realize that you carry universal love inside you. Keep charging your heart chakra. Feel the love and all the positive energies in the universe. All these, are now in your heart.

Relax. Now exercise some love, let go of the ray of light, and let it descend down to your solar plexus chakra. This is the center of your will. The more you charge this chakra, the stronger your willpower becomes. Like a sponge, absorb the energy from the ray of white light. See your solar plexus chakra get stronger. It is glowing. The more you feed it with energy, the more it glows. Keep charging it, so that you can have a will of steel. You are strong.

Gently, direct the light to flow down to your sacral chakra. This is your sex chakra, the realm of sexuality. See the ray of light charging your sex chakra. Do you see how much the orange color of your sex chakra is growing? Imagine being engaged in a hot, steamy, lovemaking session. Feel the arousal and the passion. Do you like it? Shift your focus back to the ray of light. See and feel how it charges your sex chakra.

Finally, let the ray of light descend down to your root chakra. Remember that this chakra's color is red, and it signifies security and safety. The more you charge this aura, the more grounded and secure you will become. Feel how the ray of divine light charges your root chakra. Nothing is impossible for this divine light. The more it charges you, the more centered and grounded you become. You are one with Mother Earth. Keep charging. See the red color glowing brightly. It is blinding. You are safe.

Slowly, see and feel the divine ray of light return back to heaven. From your root chakra, feel it move up slowly to your energized sacral chakra, then slowly up your powerful solar plexus chakra, gently up to your loving heart chakra, and slowly to your throat chakra. Gently, see the ray of light withdraw upwards to your all-seeing third eye chakra, and then as it leaves through your crown chakra, smile and thank the divine ray of light from heaven. Watch it move up to heaven and slowly disappear.

Keep your eyes closed. See and feel the seven main chakras of your body glowing brightly. You are strong, powerful, and healthy. You are divine. Place your hands on your chest, inhale slowly — and as you inhale, imagine inhaling the energy of love and kindness. Exhale gently. Say your thanks to the universe, and slowly open your eyes.

Inner light meditation *(Duration: at least 10 minutes)*

This is another interesting meditation technique, where you only need to focus on the *light*. Try not to fall asleep. The steps are as follows:

1. Close your eyes.

2. Relax.

3. Gently focus on the *light*. Everything that you see that is not *black* is considered light.

4. If visions appear, then shift your attention and focus on the visions.

5. Simply relax and let go.

(Give this meditation technique at least 10 minutes.)

6. Gently, think of your physical body. Slowly move your toes, and then your fingers. Slowly, open your eyes.

Spirit guide meditation *(Duration: at least 30 minutes)*

It is believed that every person has a spirit guide. A spirit guide is someone who looks after your spiritual development and guides you in your spiritual journey. Some people call it a guardian angel. This meditation will allow you to meet your spirit guide and bond with him or her. The steps are as follows:

Imagine yourself standing in front of your physical body. See your physical body still and meditating. Look at your face, your shoulders, and your feet. You look safe, beautiful, and relaxed. Now, look at the room and all the things around you. You are outside your body, yet you and the universe continue to exist.

Slowly walk to your door. Open it. When opening the door, you see a vast forest in front of you. See the trees and the grass just outside your door. Know that if you step on the grass, you will be transported into another dimension — a realm where everything is possible. Your spirit guide is waiting for you in the forest. If you sincerely want to meet your spirit guide, then take a step.

Feel the grass below your feet. Feel the air blowing, and hear the leaves shaken by the wind. Walk into the forest. Maintain a straight path, so that you can easily find your way back later. What do you see? Are there animals around? Continue to walk into the forest. Do you hear the birds chirping?

As you journey deep into the forest, you see a large clearing in front of you. In the center of the clearing stands your spirit guide smiling at you. What does your spirit guide look like? Is your guide a male or a female? Is it even human? A spirit guide can be any form: human, animal, plant, or even just a ball of energy. Just be open to anything and see.

Approach your guide and greet him. Now, feel free to talk with your guide about anything. If you want, you can take a walk in the forest or just stay in the clearing and enjoy your moment together. Most of the time, guides communicate telepathically, so you might get impressions, thoughts, and images, from your guide. Take a moment now with your guide.

The sun begins to set and your guide escorts you back to the door that leads to your room. Thank your guide and enter your room.

Watch your body in the room. It is time to get back into your body. Simply will yourself back and enter your body. Now, slowly move your toes, then your fingers. And gently, open your eyes.

Healing meditation *(Duration: at least 15 minutes)*

Take as much time as you can when you do this meditation. It is important to not just visualize the light, but you should also feel its healing quality. Of course, faith is also important.

Assume a meditative position. Make sure that your spine is straight and that you are relaxed. Imagine a brilliant ray of white light descends from the heavens. It is a divine healing light. Anything and everything that it touches gets healed and rejuvenated. Now, see and feel it enter the top of your head. Slowly, it fills your entire head. Feel the strong, powerful healing energy. Let it descend down your throat, and then down your chest and shoulders. Let the intense healing light fill every space. Feel and absorb the healing energy. Now, let the light descend down your arms, to your hands. Let it flow down your stomach, then gently down your legs, until your whole body is covered with intense, white healing light. Keep charging yourself with this healing energy. The more you charge yourself, the stronger you glow.

Once you are ready to end the meditation, simply imagine the ray of light slowly disappears. Thank the universe, and then gently open your eyes. You are healed.

Walking meditation

Although meditation is usually practiced while sitting or lying down, some meditation techniques are done in a standing position, or even while walking. A good example of this is the walking meditation. It is good to do this meditation when you go out for a stroll. The steps are simple: Simply walk around but be conscious every movement. You may want to start slow, and then gradually increase the pace as you get used to it. Surprising as it may be, you might just appreciate how wonderful the simple act of walking can be. Just like other meditations, you should be able to clear your mind and simply focus on your walk. Take note that you should focus on the act of moving and not on the surrounding scene. Therefore, feel how your feet touch and leave the floor, as well as how you breathe as you move. Feel every movement and just relax. If your thoughts start to wonder, just stop and relax for a while, and then simply start over again. If you want some light exercise, then going for a walking meditation can be your best choice. In fact, you can also do this when you go to the mall to buy something.

CHAPTER 3

Common Pitfalls

Here are the common pitfalls that beginners make when they meditate. It is best that you pay careful attention to each of them so that you will not commit the same mistakes.

Expectations

Having expectations can ruin a meditation. When you meditate, you should not expect anything to happen; otherwise, your focus and energy will be divided. For example, when you do a breathing meditation, simply focus on your breathing, and do not think of getting any sense of peace or calmness. Allow things to unfold as they are without you controlling them. A common pitfall with regard to having expectations is forcing yourself not to expect. When this happens, your focus divided. The solution here is simply not to care about what will happen. Simply do the steps of the meditation technique that you are using without any regard as to what may happen.

Analyzing

This is a common mistake committed by almost all beginners. It is important that you do not analyze anything when you meditate. This is also the reason why it is important to know the steps even before you engage in the actual practice of meditation. When you meditate, everything should flow naturally. Never analyze whether what you are doing is correct or not. Otherwise, you will end up analyzing and not meditating. Some meditators advice that you should not research so much about the meditation technique that you want to use, because sometimes having too much knowledge can be a disadvantage, especially if you still have not achieved a good level of spirituality.

Wrong posture

Maintaining a proper form or posture is important in meditation. Whether you meditate while sitting or lying down, the important thing is to keep your spine straight. This is to ensure a steady and smoother flow of energy in the body.

No slouching. Make sure that your seven main chakras are aligned. It is worth noting that there are some meditation techniques that can be done even without assuming the recommended posture. However, such kind of meditation techniques is rare.

Meditating when sleepy

It is not recommended to meditate when you are sleepy. This is because you can easily fall asleep. When you are sleepy, it is a sign that your body needs to rest, and there is no better rest than having a good sleep. If you always feel sleepy when meditating, try to meditate in the morning just a few minutes after you wake up.

Although you can also meditate at night before bed, it is not good when you are too tired. Do not worry; just continuously meditate and you will get better at it.

Another reason why meditating in bed may not always be a good choice is because the bed signals sleep to your body. That is why many meditators pick to not use their bed when they meditate. But, this is a matter of personal preference. There are also those who meditate while sitting or lying in their bed and get good results.

Meditating right after eating

It is not recommended to meditate right after eating. This is because the body functions and uses energy to digest the food. When you meditate, every part of your body should be still and relaxed, and all your energy must be devoted to meditation. The energy body has many spiritual nerves, and these nerves get heavy after eating a big meal, which will prevent you from reaching a high state of consciousness. When you meditate at the right time, you will usually feel your body get lighter and lighter; however, when you meditate after a big meal, your energy body also tend to get "heavy," and it will be hard for you to reach a higher state of mind. So, it is recommended that you meditate on an empty stomach.

Mornings are excellent for this. But, you can also meditate after about two hours from your last meal. If hunger bothers you when meditating, you can try to eat or drink something light, such as a glass of milk, a small cookie, or a glass of juice.

Focus on *focusing*

This is a common problem usually faced by beginners. Take note that there is a difference between focusing on your mantra and focusing on focusing on your mantra. When you focus on your mantra, you do not even think about focusing. Instead, your mind gets filled with the mantra.

To focus means to bring your attention to something, and you can do this with the mere exercise of the will. It is worth noting that when meditating, your focus should be relaxed, without any pressure or tension. How long you can remain focused also matter. Some people

Ego

To progress in meditation, there must be a destruction of the ego. It is important that you forget who you are or what you are good at, and *just be*. Ego is one of the things that hinder spiritual development. Learn to drop your ego and submit your whole self to your mantra.

A good way to deal with the ego is simply to drop it and not give it any attention. Also, stay humble even when you notice some developments. Know that there is still a long way ahead of you. Meditation is also not a competition on which one is holier. You do not have to compare yourself with others. Meditation is a personal journey — a spiritual pilgrimage.

Ego is not just an obstacle during meditation. It is also a hindrance to spiritual development. It is worth noting, however, that dropping your ego is not the same as lack of confidence. Having confidence is good, but too much of it is not.

Never compare yourself with others, especially when you experience spiritual developments. If you do compare, then compare your progress with those who have a higher state of spirituality than you. Ego is a tricky thing. Stay humble; stay true; stay pure.

Fasting

Fasting is not always a bad thing. In fact, it is also healthy.

However, fasting can make it harder for you to focus. It is simply hard to focus on something when you are feeling very hungry. For beginners, fasting is not advisable. You must try to be as relaxed and comfortable as you can. Take note that fasting is not necessary.

Focusing on the visions

When you meditate, visions will start to appear. When this happens, simply focus on your mantra, except if the meditation technique that you use is really meant trigger some visions. Although it is easy to get tempted to focus on the visions instead since they may seem to be magical, such is not a good practice because it will not advance your spiritual development.

Some people may confuse these visions with lucid dreaming, or the ability to be conscious in one's dreams. Although this is possible when one meditates, there are different other visions and experiences that you may encounter. Again, just remember to focus on your mantra or the main point of the meditation technique that you are using.

Depending on meditation

It is wrong to depend too much on meditation. Some people use meditation as an excuse for mere laziness or irresponsibility. Some things in life cannot be solved just by meditating. For example, if you have financial problems, meditating even the whole day and night will not earn you any money. Remember that meditation is a spiritual pilgrimage and not a way to be lazy and irresponsible. Some people think that they progress spiritually by simply doing meditation and nothing else. Just think about it: What use is spirituality if you have no time to love or be loved by someone? What use is being compassionate if you distance yourself from people who need compassion?

Doubts

Doubts in the meditation technique that you are using, especially doubt in yourself, can ruin your meditation. Have faith and never doubt. If you should doubt a particular technique or anything else, entertain your doubts after meditation. But, during meditation, you must let go of doubts and simply be present in the moment of Now.

Once you entertain doubts, you will get divided and it will be impossible to achieve a higher state if consciousness. Also, doubting shifts your mindset into an analytical state of mind, which is not good for any form of meditation. When you meditate, you should let go of everything, especially your doubts.

Worrying

Some beginners usually worry while meditating. They feel itchy and their legs feel numb after some minutes of being engaged in meditation. It should be noted that the practice of meditation is safe. When you feel your legs get numbed, which usually happens when you meditate in a cross-legged position, it is nothing to worry about because it is normal. In fact, the deeper you go into meditation, the more you will not feel your physical body — where literally nothing will exist but your mantra. Needless to say, feeling some parts of your body getting itchy is also normal and is something that you should not allow yourself to get distracted with.

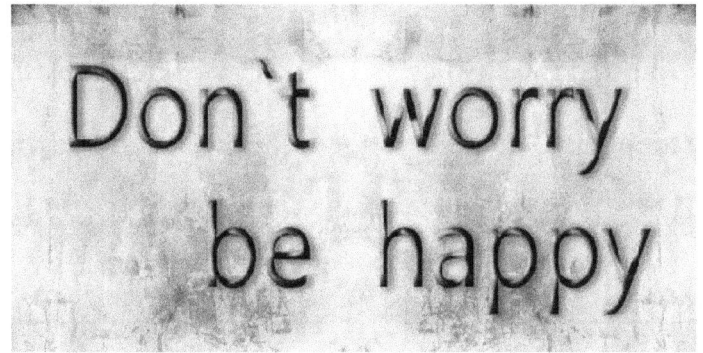

Of course, worry may come in the form of your real-life problems, for example, money problems or relationship problems. Although you should deal with such problems, you should understand that the time for doing meditation is not the time to think of such problems. Do not worry; you have all the time to think of those problems *after* meditation. But, during meditation, only focus on your mantra and still your mind.

Negative thoughts

Avoid negative thoughts. In fact, never entertain any negative thought. This is true whether you are engaged in actual meditation or not. Of course, this does not mean that you will be blind to any form of negativity. Rather, this simply means that you notice any negative thoughts but do not cling to any of them. According to ancient teachings in alchemy, the proper way to deal with negative thoughts is not to deal with them directly. Instead, you should just focus on the opposite, which is the positive side. For example, if you have thoughts that make you sad, then think and do things that will make you happy. By doing so, the negative energy will disappear on its own.

Another effective way to deal with negativity is to use affirmations. For example, if you think that you cannot do any meditation properly because you do not feel at peace due to lots of random thoughts, you can use an affirmation that will give you the right and positive mindset. For example, you can use the affirmation, "I am at peace." or "I meditate peacefully."

You can make your own affirmation. The key is to use the present moment and believe what you are saying. Now, the matter of believing what you are saying may be difficult. After all, how can you believe something that you say that you know is just some form of wishful thinking and that the present reality is different? The key is to realize that what you say is possible, that it is all a matter of the mind. Therefore, if you adopt the right mindset, then it is no longer just wishful thinking but creates reality.

When it comes to making affirmations, there are a few points to consider: You must believe whatever it is that you affirm or say. You affirmation must be in the present tense. Last but not least, you must continue to do the affirmation until it works. Now, the third point should be qualified. Most people keep saying their affirmation on a regular basis, which means that they chant it many times. However, other people only mention their affirmation only once. Now, take note that both ways are correct and effective. The reason here is the presence and power of faith. Most beginners have to mention their affirmation many times before their mind can be influenced and take the proper mindset, while some advanced practitioners only need to mention it once, and they can already change their mindset. So, to avoid confusion, simply do what works for you.

It is not easy to avoid negative thoughts. They are simply very pushy and are good at getting one's attention. This is where self-mastery comes into play. Again, a good way to have self-mastery is also by persevering in your meditation practices.

The dark side of the mind usually reveals itself by bombarding you with negative thoughts. It will either make lots of negative thoughts to arise in your mind or simply use one or two negative thoughts that are extremely effective in distracting you. Either way, you will be faced with a big challenge of focusing on your mantra despite the great and very tempting distractions of the mind.

The mind is a very tricky thing. It is not uncommon for it to show you the strongest negative thought that you will find hard to ignore. The key to success when you encounter this is simply to stay true to your meditation. The more you allow yourself to be affected, the more you will lose focus. Unfortunately, some people at this point simply feel that they are not good enough to have any more progress and just drop their meditation practices thinking that they will never improve anymore. This is wrong. When the mind gets this tricky, you should have all the more reasons to stay strong. Although this may be a difficult stage to get pass through, you will usually experience a good reward in the form of bliss once you succeed it. The key is not to give up and continue on meditating. Instead of focusing on such negative thought or thoughts, simply be strong enough and focus on your meditation practice. The negative thought will not disappear right away, but if you do not pay any attention to it and just focus on your mantra, the said negative energy will disappear on its own — and you will be surprised just how much development you have achieved.

CHAPTER 4

Keys To Success

Here are some keys to success that will allow you to enjoy the best benefits of practicing meditation:

Continuous practice

Continuous practice is the key to meditation. As much as possible, try to meditate every day. Although you can practice different kinds of meditation, you should have one meditation technique that you should always practice. In meditation, the power of repetition is also important. So, be sure to meditate regularly. Among all the keys to success, this advice is the most important.

Develop your concentration

If you want to succeed in meditation, you need to have good concentration. Concentration simply refers to being able to focus on something without being distracted. Obviously, this is how all meditations should be — where you exist and experience the present moment and not get distracted. Most people care able to concentrate for a few seconds or minutes, but then notice that their mind starts to bombard itself with random thoughts after some time. If you are one of such people, then there is nothing for you to worry about because it is normal. Be kind and gentle to yourself and simply continue practicing. Regular practice of meditation naturally improves concentration. Another effective way to improve your concentration is by staring at an object. When you do, let nothing exist in your mind or consciousness but the object you are staring at. You can use any object that you want. It can be a pen, your mobile phone, or even your door frame. Do this for ten seconds, and then gradually increase the time. Stop when a thought that is not related to the object arises in the mind. Just give yourself maybe a few seconds to rest, and then start over. Be sure to do this regularly. You can also do this technique almost anytime and anywhere by simply closing your eyes and imagining the object.

Be one with the mantra

You need to have mastery of your mantra in order to be one with it. Once you have chosen a mantra that you want to use, keep saying it consciously, out loud or even just in your mind. Through continuous repetition, even your subconscious mind will get to know your mantra. In the beginning, when you meditate, you may have to put effort in saying your mantra. But, once you get used to your mantra, it will come naturally. In fact, you would not even have to chant it anymore. Instead, you will "hear" it being chanted on its own, and all that you have to do is close your eyes and meditate.

Another benefit if a mantra meditation is that you can use your mantra to trigger a pleasant state of mind even during normal or waking consciousness. For example, when you are feeling down or confused, simply chant your mantra, and you may notice feeling a glimpse of that bliss that you get when you meditate, which can help you get through a rough day. Of course, for this to work, you must have established a strong connection with your mantra.

Let go

When you meditate, you must learn to let go. Let go and free your soul. To let go also means to let go of any expectations and even beliefs. To simply be, without preferences or prejudices. Let go of what you want to happen. Instead, experience the present moment.

Live healthy

As mentioned in the first chapter of this book, the state of your energy body affects your physical body. It is also worth noting that the state of your physical body also affects your energy body. Therefore, it is important that you keep your physical body healthy. Learn to love healthy and follow a healthy diet.

Exercising is also good. In fact, doing physical exercises naturally strengthens your energy body. You do not have to be very fit to do this. You do not need to have six-pack abs. By simply improving your diet and living healthy, all your energy bodies, including your physical body, will also develop.

Introspection

Introspection or understanding one's self is important in meditation. The more you can understand yourself, the more you can control your thoughts. This is the time that you should judge yourself without any bias or prejudice. The important thing here is to be very honest with yourself. Although not necessary, you may find it helpful to use a journal to record your day-to-day meditation experiences, especially the challenges that you encounter. Do not worry; you do not have to be a professional writer to do this. Again, the important thing is for you to write as honest as you can. Keeping a journal will also allow you to think outside the box and see yourself from a different perspective. By doing so, you can get to think more clearly and understand yourself better.

When you do introspection, you have to identify your strengths and weaknesses. The objective is to increase your strengths and develop your weaknesses. This is why being brutally honest is important. Your journal should be a mirror of your soul. Unfortunately, many meditators do not accept their weaknesses. Just remember that the more honest you are in understanding yourself and in writing your journal, the better it will be for your development.

When engaged in introspection, think of the "mistakes" that you often encounter. Are there certain thoughts that keep repeating themselves in your mind? Try to find out why and what you can do to improve.

On a more spiritual note, the art of meditation is actually a deep sense of introspection. The practice of meditation will make you realize who you really are, as well as the oneness of everything else.

Learn to deal with distractions

It is worth noting that being distracted even during meditation is normal. Just as your body releases sweat or feels itchy, your mind releases so many thoughts. Just as sweating is a natural and important for the body, you should not see your thoughts as an enemy. Remember that before you can reach a state of no-mind, you must first be in a state where many thoughts are present. Be gentle and make peace with your thoughts by realizing that your thoughts are not an enemy. It is how you handle your thoughts that matter.

When distractions arise in the mind, you must remain calm and non-judgmental. Simply focus on your mantra or any point of focus of your meditation. You should not deal with distractions by being distracted. Rather, you conquer every distraction by simply doing the right thing.

Change

Do not be afraid to change. Regular practice of meditation can change a person for the better. As you continue to practice meditation, you may notice that you feel calmer and more focused. Remember that there is no development without a change, so learn to embrace positive changes in your life.

If the practice of meditation only makes you feel better but does not improve your personality, then you are not doing it right. All forms of meditation should make you a better person. Remember to always welcome positive changes in your life.

Continuous improvement

Always strive for continuous improvement. Even when you get good at meditating, do not stop doing introspection or looking for other ways to be better at meditating. A good way to get inspiration is to read and watch how Buddhist monks practice meditation. Also, pay attention to the discipline that they exercise. You can find many of these stories and videos online. Take note, however, that you should not view meditation as a form of competition. You do not compete against other meditators. Have you seen a saint saying or thinking that he is holier than another person? No, meditation does not work that way. Remember that meditation is a personal and spiritual pilgrimage.

Mindfulness

By intentionally focusing and fixing your attention on a fixed point, awareness increases and the mind becomes still. Also, you should not be judgmental of the moment. Instead, just accept everything as they truly are. Like a child, look at and feel everything as if it was the first time for you to experience anything. As you meditate, you may experience different states of awareness. In fact, even your emotions could change. In the midst of these changes, strive to keep an open mind. Just be conscious, and do not judge anything. Let everything unfold as they are; accept them as they are. Be mindful without intervening or being judgmental.

Although technically conscious and awake, most people are unconscious as to what happens from moment to moment. Unfortunately, for many, life has turned into a routine where every movement, breath, or second, is left unappreciated. Many get lost in their own thoughts that they fail to live and experience the present moment. As you practice meditation, you will be more aware and more present. What is more, you will be able to live this awareness and appreciation of life even after your actual practice of meditation. The more you practice mindfulness, the more you will be present in the moment of *Now*, which is the moment of being alive.

Keep it simple

Meditation is supposed to be easy and natural. Avoid doing meditations that have complex instructions; otherwise, you will end up analyzing and not meditating. Breathing and mantra meditations are simple and very effective. In fact, many monks spend years just meditating on their breath. It is also possible to achieve enlightenment even with the simplest meditation.

Detachment

Being detached is important in meditation. This means that you should be detached from your desires, ego, and even your thoughts and emotions. Detachment becomes easy when you realize that you are not the body nor the emotions nor the thoughts and that everyone and everything are connected. This is the oneness of spirituality. Of course, meditation is also the key to this realization.

Detachment also applies to your relationship with other people. You must be able to love without being too attached. Now, do not take this in a wrong way. You can and should love as much as you can. However, do not be selfish. Being so attached often leads to exercising undue control over the person you love. You should love a person as he or she is, and unconditionally. This is the secret to loving freely and without limitation. By detaching yourself from the one you love, you will be able to love him or her even more.

Understand your emotions

When you find that certain emotions are hard to ignore and prevents you from going deep into meditation, the best way to understand your emotions is to go directly to their roots. Unfortunately, many people are controlled by their emotions rather than the other way around. Most experiences in life give rise to various opportunities for emotions to take over one's life. Many think that emotions are what comprises their identity, and makes them who they are, which is wrong. Some people would think that it is okay to be angry or sad when someone has hurt them. Although logically normal, when you allow this, it creates a domino effect and makes you a slave to your own emotions, as well as the circumstances that give rise to such emotions.

It is worth noting that emotions are like thoughts that come and go. Just as you already know that you are not your thoughts, you should also realize that you are not your emotions. Now, you should consider this as good news, especially if your emotions are the ones causing you turmoil or suffering. This does not mean that emotions are bad. Like thoughts, emotions can always be used in your favor as long as you are able to control them.

The best way to control your emotions is to find out what has caused specific emotions to arise in your mind. Most negative emotions spring from anger, jealousy, envy, and others. What you should realize about these causes is that they cannot control you unless you allow them to take over your life. Most of the time, just by not acting or responding to such stimuli, you can avoid the harsh feelings that you experience with negative emotions. Also, emotions usually depend on one's experiences. By living a good and happy life, negative emotions can be minimized. In the face of challenges, where people act badly, the key to controlling your emotions is to exercise compassion. Remember that if someone does something wrong to you, it only reflects his own sadness. It should also be noted that according to Buddhist teachings, the mind is naturally pure.

Be kind

Being kind is a good way to easily increase one's vibration. Therefore, be kind at all times. The exercise of kindness is also a good way to increase your willpower, especially at times when being kind is simply not easy to do. For example, how can you be kind to someone who keeps on insulting you? But, be kind, anyway. If you are able to exercise kindness to a person who is mean, then you will be more easily able to express kindness to your loved ones.

When you meditate with kindness in your heart, you can easily tap a higher state of consciousness. Take note that you can never achieve enlightenment is you continue to harbor any form of hatred in your heart. Therefore, learn to exercise some compassion.

How to overcome the *self*

To reach higher states of consciousness, one needs to conquer the self. The self is full of desires and ego. Hence, to overcome the self, you need to overcome your desires by not clinging to them. When desire disappears, the ego also disappears. But desire is a tricky word. Does desire to improve in meditation and be enlightened considered bad? It does not mean that it is bad, but such desire will get in the way of your spiritual development. Remember that in meditation, nothing should exist but the point of your focus. If it is a mantra meditation, then only the mantra should exist. If you meditate on your breath, then only your breath should exist. If you follow the pathworking meditation in this book, then all your focus should be devoted to that, too. You must not desire anything else but simply "to be." Given the said example, say as you meditate, you also think of achieving enlightenment, your energy will be divided, and you cannot reach a stage where nothing exists but your mantra.

Compassion

If you read books on Buddhism, you will notice that the value of compassion is always given a special importance. However, this type of compassion is not something that is demanded or forced. Such compassion must be expressed with the heart. But, to do so, there must be realization. You simply cannot be truly compassionate when evil or anger broods in your heart. As usual, the key to developing compassion is to meditate regularly.

In Buddhism, compassion is a state of mind where you cherish other beings and sincerely wish for them to be freed from suffering.

This, however, does not just mean a mere concern. For example, when your friend gets sick, you may wish for him to feel better, so you can play with him again. Now, this is not compassion. True compassion is about cherishing others, even without receiving any benefit from it. In today's world, the idea of compassion is a bit narrow and biased. In Buddhism, compassion takes a universal form, whether one experiences something bad or good. It is a sincere desire for another to achieve enlightenment and be completely free from suffering. Universal compassion can be attained through years of intense training.

Meditation is life

Meditation should not distance you from people, especially from your loved ones. Although many people these days meditate to relieve stress and feel better, the true effects of meditation are not really just for yourself, but also for others. Meditation should lead you to be kinder, express more love, and exercise compassion at all times. You must do so sincerely. The fact remains that even among those who meditate for years, only a few reach enlightenment in one lifetime. Therefore, although enlightenment may be your goal on why you meditate, never allow yourself to be obsessed with the idea of enlightenment. If you want to have less stress and live a happier life, then make peace with the people around you and show your love, even to your enemies. Meditation will give you the strength that you need to do so. All forms of meditation also develop the heart chakra, which will allow you to be more compassionate and exercise universal love.

CHAPTER 5
Answers to Common Questions

To further assist you in your spiritual journey, here are the answers to common questions about meditation:

Is it safe to practice meditation?

Generally, it is safe to practice meditation; however, there are meditation techniques that are not completely safe. Some meditation techniques require an intense form of discipline and could damage your chakras if not performed properly. The good news is that all the meditations in this book are completely safe.

How do I get started to meditate?

The only way to get started and truly learn meditation is simply by doing it. So, start meditating. Just choose a good time and place where you will not be distracted.

How long should I meditate?

You can meditate as much as you want. You can meditate for a few minutes, and you can also meditate for more than a day if you can. It is important that you focus on the quality of your meditation.

How do I know if I am doing it right?

You should understand that there is really no right and wrong way to meditate. Simply try whatever you want and see what works best for you. If you do not notice any progress in a few weeks, then try to make some adjustments. It is good to listen to your body and intuition.

How can I tell if I have achieved a high state of consciousness?

Each level has certain characteristics, which are described in the book. It is important to note that reaching a high state of consciousness should be seen as a mere result and not as an objective; otherwise, the very purpose of meditation would be lost. Regardless whether you are a beginner or not, your purpose for meditating should not be about reaching a high state of consciousness. Such kind of consciousness will naturally reveal itself as you progress in your spiritual journey.

Is it better to meditate in the morning?

The best time to meditate depends on the person. It varies. Many people find that meditating in the morning is easier because they feel more focused and not sleepy. However, others prefer meditating at night because it feels more peaceful and quiet. This depends on you and your lifestyle. If you want, you can meditate both in the morning and in the evening.

Should I use the same place for meditation?

Having one place where you meditate helps to focus the mind. By simply going to that place, it automatically signals the mind that it is time to meditate. However, this is not required. You can meditate anywhere you want. You might want to try different spots and see which one feels most comfortable for you.

Should I close my eyes when I meditate?

Again, this is a matter of personal preference. Many choose eto close those eyes to minimize distractions and to help them be more focused. Closing your eyes is also helpful when you engage in a pathworking meditation or where you need to imagine vivid sceneries. However, if you are comfortable meditating with your eyes open, then feel free to do that as well.

How long does it take to experience the benefits of meditation?

There is no hard and fast rule to this. You can already experience some benefits even if it is your first time to meditate. Other people usually experience the benefits after a few days. Meditating properly takes some practice. However, once you get the hang of it, you can experience the benefits of meditation every time you meditate, and even after meditation.

Will the practice of meditation give me psychic powers?

Yes. Meditation develops the chakras, which energizes your psychic senses. It is not uncommon for advanced meditators to share mystical and psychic experiences including being able to perform some magical feats. However, it should be noted that obtaining psychic powers should not be the purpose of your meditation. Also, such psychic powers only manifest when you reach a high level of spirituality and a natural effect of having highly developed chakras and a strong energy body.

Is meditation different from relaxation?

Yes. Relaxation is simply one of the common effects of meditation. Meditation can be considered a spiritual journey and is an active process where you remain aware and conscious of what you are doing. Meditation also offers more benefits than mere passive relaxation.

Is meditation against my religion?

Meditation is not barred by any religion. In fact, all the major religions in the world have their own meditation practices. Meditation is normal in spirituality. In fact, it can even be considered a need.

What is the best way to meditate?

There is no such thing as the better or best way to meditate. All forms of meditation lead to the same thing, which is enlightenment. Therefore, use the one that you think works best for you. If there were such thing as the best way, then that is simply to meditate as often as you can. Meditation is a life-long journey.

Any last tips?

Start meditating and persevere. I strongly recommend that you focus on learning the breathing or mantra meditation. You can also use other meditation techniques from time to time. Persevere and try to meditate every day. If you are a very busy person, you may find meditating at night as the best time to meditate. However, should you meditate at night, it is recommended that you do not meditate while lying down because it can easily trigger you to feel sleepy, especially when you are already tired after the day's work.

To learn more about meditation, it is good to read books on Buddhism and Hinduism. These spiritual paths hold the practice of meditation of great importance. You should also learn the teachings of Buddha.

To be a better meditator, cultivate a good and loving heart. Keep in mind that only those with a pure heart and mind can enter the highest states of consciousness. To have a good heart and mind, learn from your loved ones and from your enemies. Your loved ones will encourage you to love, while your enemies will teach you many important values.

Do not be too hard on yourself. The practice of meditation is not supposed to be hard. It must come naturally, without any tension or pressure.

If you can, try to learn to meditate in the evening just before going to sleep, so that you will not have to worry about the time. When meditating, it is easy to lose track of time, especially when you go deep into the meditation.

If you are interested in mantra meditation, then learn to be one with your mantra. Chant your mantra even when not meditating. Let it seep into your soul that you can hear it echo on its own. When you reach this kind of connection with your mantra, you only need to close your eyes to "hear" it. This means that you no longer have to physically chant it over and over again, which will allow you to focus on it even more. Also, avoid changing your mantra. When you change your mantra, you will have to work on building a connection with it over again.

It is also helpful to find befriend people who are also interested in meditation. This will help boost your interest, and can also be a good way to learn more about meditation. Also, practicing meditation is a group makes it easier to reach a higher state of consciousness. This is because of the effect of the group consciousness that is formed. Just be sure that the people that you meditate with are truly passionate and interested in meditation.

You should also realize that meditation is only a part of spirituality and that spirituality does not refer to meditation alone. Here is the secret: Spirituality is life. Live a good life, surround yourself with people who love you and love them without end, and you will have the best spirituality you can ever ask for.

CONCLUSION

Thank you for making it through to the end of this book. I hope it was informative and able to provide you with all of the tools you need to achieve your goals, whatever they may be.

The next step is to start trying some of these techniques in your life and find out what works best for you.

Finally, if you found this book useful in any way, a review on Amazon is always appreciated! -Sarah Rowland

DESCRIPTION

Meditation for Beginners: Ultimate Guide to Relieve Stress, Depression, and Anxiety is your one-stop guide that will teach you everything that you need to know about meditation.

Learn:

- What meditation is
- The basics of meditation
- Different meditation techniques
- To use meditation to relieve stress, anxiety, and depression
- The different states of consciousness
- Common pitfalls
- Keys to success

And so much more!

This book is the handy manual that will change your life and free yourself from negative energies. *NOW* is the time to make a change and live a happier life.

MINDFULNESS FOR BEGINNERS

Ultimate Guide To Achieve Happiness by Eliminating Stress, Depression and Anxiety

Sarah Rowland

INTRODUCTION

Mindfulness is a practice that has a powerful ability to teach people to develop a sense of self-awareness and understanding. When you develop a mindfulness practice, you give yourself the opportunity to learn more about your inner self and how you operate with the world around you.

"Mindfulness for Beginners: Ultimate Guide to Achieve Happiness by Eliminating Stress, Anxiety, and Depression" is a guide that will teach you how to master mindfulness and take control over your life once and for all. Every day, people suffer from stress, anxiety and depression. The suffering is often prolonged because people are unaware about how they can deal with their own internal responses to these emotions, therefore they attempt to repress them or they take actions which make them worse.

In this guide, you are going to learn how you can master the art and transform your life. While mindfulness will not eliminate the experiences of stress, anxiety and depression, it certainly will help you learn how you can gain control over these emotions and work through them effectively and in a way that serves you.

Throughout this book you are going to learn about the value of mindfulness, as well as be guided through specific strategies that will help you practice mindfulness in your own life. You will 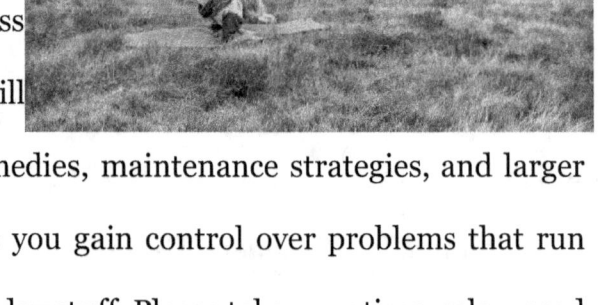 learn about instant remedies, maintenance strategies, and larger practices that will help you gain control over problems that run deeper than the day-to-day stuff. Please take your time, relax, read at your own pace, and enjoy!

CHAPTER 1

The Power Of Mindfulness

Mindfulness practices have been taught for decades. The lessons of mindfulness teach us to explore our inner worlds on a deeper level, which provides us with a greater sense of self-awareness. As a result, we learn how to masterfully work together with our emotions to achieve a higher level of peace in life.

What is Mindfulness?

While nearly everyone is talking about it, many people are unclear as to what mindfulness is exactly. In the bigger picture, mindfulness is exactly what you may think: a deeper sense of self-awareness that teaches you all about how you interact with the world around you and within' you.

On a smaller scale, however, mindfulness is many things. It is the series of strategies you use to develop that greater sense of self-awareness. It is also the exact moment when you stop reacting and start recognizing how you feel and the present moment and start responding to it. Mindfulness is an on-going practice that you must work on regularly to maintain it. While you can achieve mindfulness, you cannot maintain it if you don't work towards it. You will have to continually learn to balance yourself in order to achieve mindfulness for a long period of time. Some days it will be easier than others, some days you might feel as though you've failed altogether. The reality is that as long as you are having these regular check ins, then you are doing exactly what you need to be doing to maintain your mindfulness practice.

How Does Mindfulness Help Stress, Anxiety and Depression?

There are three levels where mindfulness assists with reducing and eliminating stress, anxiety and depression. Each of these levels will be available in every instance of the aforementioned emotions, but you might only realize your "window of opportunity" in one of them. They are: before, during, and after. Regardless of where you find your opportunity to start practicing mindfulness, the main point is that you start.

Before

Having a regular, on-going mindfulness maintenance practice can significantly reduce levels of stress, anxiety and depression. Because of your frequent check-ins and practices, you will likely find that you pay greater attention to your body and therefore you are able to deal with certain internal (or external) circumstances before they evolve into anything significant. As a result, you will be able to prevent yourself from having the added stress, anxiety and depression that many people accumulate by ignoring their bodies.

During

People who maintain a regular mindfulness practice are able to recognize when they are experiencing symptoms of stress, anxiety or depression. Because of this, they are able to recognize that these emotions are merely emotional responses to events in life, and that they are not doomed to feeling this way forever. These people are also equipped with tools to assist them with reducing and eliminating these emotions because they are able to practice mindfulness and transition their mind back into a peaceful place by mindfully working through the present emotions.

After

Sometimes, even extremely mindful people may not be able to recognize that they are beginning to experience symptoms of stress, anxiety or depression. Instead, they notice after the symptoms have already been around for a while. This is completely natural and experienced often by people. It does not mean that you have failed or that it is too late. Instead, it means that you simply need to practice your mindfulness strategies and regain control over the situation by developing your peace.

Regardless of when you recognize symptoms of various emotions creeping up on you, the best thing you can do is respond with mindful practices. It is important that you refrain from beating yourself up over not recognizing the symptoms sooner. Over time, you will become more self-aware and eventually it will be easier for you to recognize the symptoms quickly. However, there will always be times where you may struggle more than others. Remember, mindfulness is a practice that must be practiced regularly in order for it to be maintained.

Mindfulness for Other Emotions

Mindfulness is not restricted to only assisting with reducing and eliminating feelings of stress, anxiety and depression. Having a regular mindfulness practice can aid with many different things in life. You can use it to increase peace and happiness in your life. You can also use it to decrease anger, sadness, and other uncomfortable emotions that you will not want to experience for prolonged periods of time.

It is important to understand that mindfulness is not the same as repression. The key is not to identify unwanted emotions and then repress them in order to replace them with wanted emotions. Instead, mindfulness is an indirect approach to effectively deal with the situation. When you are mindful, you are able to gather a large amount of information around your circumstances and use that to your advantage. You can use it to effectively work through emotions you are experiencing by facing them head on and letting yourself heal through them. As a result, you will then be able to experience a greater sense of peace and happiness. Mindfulness is not the practice of replacing emotions, rather it is the practice of working through them.

Empowering Your Mindfulness Practice

It is important to understand how a mindfulness practice should work. The second word of the experience is "practice", because it is something that you need to practice regularly. When you establish a mindfulness practice, you can empower it by spending time enhancing your skill and continuing the exploration of your inner self. The more you invest into your mindfulness practice, the more powerful it will become and the greater value you will gain from it. Mindfulness is not a practice that is meant to be accomplished and then forgotten about. Instead, mindfulness is a lifelong journey where you continually delve deeper into yourself and learn more and more about yourself along the way.

Empowering your mindfulness practice is simple. You simply must believe in it, practice regularly, and allow yourself to nurture it enough so that it will grow. By doing this, you will ensure that you have a strong mindfulness practice that will serve you for years to come. Ideally you should take your favorite mindfulness guides, such as this one, and revisit them from time to time to ensure that you are staying on track with your practice. Guides like this are excellent for beginners as well as those who have been practicing for a long time. Mindfulness is actually a simple practice. However, the longer we practice the more complex we may make it out to be. The best thing you can do is make sure that you are keeping it light and focusing on the foundation of the practice. The rest will take care of itself as a result.

Mindfulness is a powerful practice that allows people to explore the depths of their inner world. When you practice mindfulness, you gain the ability to learn more about yourself than ever before. Instead of reacting to your inner and outer circumstances, you will learn to respond. You will also gain a greater sense of self-awareness that will allow you to know how you feel and think at all times. This means that you will have a greater opportunity to change the way you work together with your own mind and emotions and thus have more control over your life in general. Mindfulness is not a practice that allows you to replace uncomfortable emotions with pleasant ones. Rather, it is a practice that teaches you to effectively work through the painful emotions to open up room in your life for you to welcome the pleasant ones.

CHAPTER 2

Simple Practices

When you are learning mindfulness, it is important to understand simple practices first. Then, you can build your way up from there. Simple practices are practices that take five minutes or less. You should start your journey of mindfulness by practicing one or two of these each day. Additionally, you can use these strategies whenever you recognize that you are having a moment where you are reacting to your circumstances more than you typically do. They will assist you with regathering control over the situation and responding in a way that serves your highest good.

Grounding Technique

Having a solid grounding technique available is important. Grounding allows you to become present in the moment and refrain from magnifying situations in your mind. Many times when we feel excessively emotional about particular things we have a tendency to obsess over them and make them seem bigger or worse than they really are. When you are able to effectively ground yourself from these energies and emotions, you allow yourself the ability to step back and remove yourself from this obsessive reaction. Then, you can respond with actions that will serve your highest good.

You should ground yourself at least twice a day. Once in the morning and once at night. Doing this will help you wake up and shed the stresses of the day before, and will allow you to go to bed after shedding the stresses of the day you had. Grounding is not an opportunity to eliminate unwanted emotions, rather it is an opportunity to remove yourself from the obsessive thinking part and gives you the chance to look at it from a more neutralized state of mind. You should also use your grounding strategy when you are experiencing a heightened sense of emotions that is causing you to check out of the moment and become absorbed in your mind as you obsess over events you cannot control.

To ground yourself, you want to start by standing or sitting somewhere with your feet planted firmly on the floor. Take a few moments to breathe deeply, and then start to check in with your body. You will do this by first checking in with your eyes. Take a moment to notice what your eyes feel like. Are they dry? Do they ache in behind from stress? Are you blinking more than usual? What do you notice? Once you have checked in, take a few moments to look at five things around the room. What five things do you see that catch your eye?

Next, think about your hands. What do your hands feel like? As you are looking at them, how do they look? Notice the edges against whatever background they are against. Then, take a few moments to notice four things you can touch. Don't simply touch these things, but rather take some time to explore them with your hands. What do they feel like? What is the texture? Are they warm or cold? What do you notice about them that is unique or stands out to you most? Take your time and experience each of the four things.

Now you are going to think about your ears. How do they feel? When we are stressed, anxious or depressed, sometimes our ears can feel hot. We may even hear ringing noises or notice that our environment sounds faded out as we are so absorbed in our thoughts. Take a few moments to listen to the things around you. What are three things you can hear? What do they sound like? Are they sounds you hear so often they fade into the background, or are they sounds that are new to you? What else do you notice about the sounds? Give yourself a few moments to really explore each sound and identify everything you can about it.

Next let's move onto your nose. Noses are fascinating. Even though we can see them with our eyes, our eyes are so used to them that they have learned to make them invisible to us so that we can focus on our surroundings past our nose. Take a few seconds to think about how your nose feels on your face. Sometimes when our emotions are particularly uncomfortable we can develop discomfort in our sinuses or regular itching on our faces. Do you notice any of this? If you do, take a few moments to consciously release the tension and discomfort. Then, notice two things you can smell. What are the two things? Where are they coming from? Are they pleasant, or does the smell not appeal to you? Give it a few moments as you really address these questions and recognize how these smells make you feel and where they are coming from.

Finally, we are going to consider your mouth. Take a few moments to really explore your mouth. Is it dry? If so, take a sip of water. Alternatively, do you find that you are holding your tongue in a different position because of your present emotions? Maybe you have it stuck to the roof of your mouth, or maybe you are biting it between your teeth. If so, allow yourself to relax and let your tongue rest again. When you are ready, think about something you can taste right now. If there is no outstanding flavor in your mouth, consider taking a sip of a beverage or a bite of a snack so that you can explore the flavor in your mouth. When you are done, swallow it.

Following these experiences, give yourself a few moments to breathe deeply and really feel your feet as they are planted firmly on the floor. Recognize that you are being supported by the earth and that you are exactly where you need to be in this very moment. When you are feeling relaxed and present again, you can resume your daily activities.

Having a regular grounding routine this way allows you to activate all of your five senses in a matter of minutes. When you are able to do so, you  bring your entire awareness back into the present moment. This assists with bringing you out of your mind and can help you stay focused and present in the current situation. If you find that you regularly "check out" of circumstances when you are experiencing certain emotions that may be particularly difficult or uncomfortable, it is a good idea to practice a grounding session. The session doesn't have to be long or intensive, just a few minutes of breathing and focusing on your senses can help you focus your awareness and resume your day from a more mindful state.

Short Body Scan

Short body scans are a quick scan you can do to assess your body for any tension or discomfort. If you notice any, you will want to make sure that you address it quickly and allow it to fade away.

Unlike the full body scan that you will learn in the advanced practices section, this is a quick scan that will allow you to quickly fix anything you are experiencing and move on.

You will want to practice this once per day until you learn how to do the full body scan. Once you learn the full body scan, you can replace this scan with that one. As you are getting started, however, the short body scan is sufficient. You are more than welcome to use this strategy at any time throughout the day, especially if you are experiencing a significant amount of painful or difficult emotions. In some cases, grounding yourself will not be enough and you will need to consciously release specific tensions. For those circumstances, the short body scan is an excellent tool to use.

To start the short body scan, take a few moments to get comfortable and breathe deeply. If you are in a situation where you can't get completely comfortable, simply relax as much as you can and breathe deeply. You may or may not wish to close your eyes depending on where you are. The only thing you will definitely want to have available to you is a few quick moments of silence where you do not have to actively engage with anyone or anything.

As you are breathing deeply, start doing your body scan. Imagine there is a long wand that is horizontal to the ground. The wand starts by hovering slightly above your head, and then moves down the front of you at a slow but steady pace. As it moves down, you can feel the energy moving with it. Anywhere there is tension or discomfort in your body, the wand stops momentarily and zaps it out of you. Then, it carries on as it scans towards your feet. The scan is done when the wand is just below your feet.

If you noticed any tension during this scan, you can either address it immediately or at a more appropriate time. If you are addressing it immediately, use the following instructions. If you are addressing it at a later time, ground yourself for the time being and then return to the discomfort when you have more time to work through the emotions.

To work through the emotions and tension, simply take a few moments to meditate on the discomfort. Work to discover what it is telling you and identify why the discomfort exists in the first place. There are many reasons as to why we feel these discomforts. It may be because you failed to listen to your body, or it may be because you are not working through emotions that are building up inside of you. Regardless of what it is, take a few moments and identify it. Then, let your body guide you through the process of working it out. You may need to move around and exercise, you may need to rest something or give yourself a total rest, or you may need to simply cry or experience the emotion inside of you so that it can be released and you can move on. Whatever you need to do, give yourself the permission to do it when you are in a safe place and then let yourself work through it. When you are done, you will find that you feel infinitely better as you are no longer harboring the discomfort of ignoring your personal needs.

How Are You Doing?

When you ask someone how they are doing, you are prompting them to quickly check in with themselves and then provide you with an answer. While they may automatically answer "good" thinking that's what you want to hear, it still encourages them to take a moment to think about how they are actually doing. Often, we forget to ask ourselves how we are doing and as a result our needs go unheard. It is important to establish the type of relationship with yourself where you aren't afraid to ask yourself how you are doing on a regular basis.

This practice is an extremely quick one that should be completed regularly throughout the day. You can do it first thing in the morning, last thing at night, and frequently throughout the day. The more you ask yourself how you are doing, the more you will be able to check in with yourself and treat yourself appropriately.

There is no real set up for this mindfulness strategy. You will not need to practice any deep breathing beforehand. Rather, you simply need to say "Hey, how are you doing?" to yourself. You might wish to do it in a mirror, or you might simply wish to quietly or mentally ask yourself the question. Do in a way that feels comfortable for you. Then, allow yourself to genuinely answer the question. Based on whatever your answers are, you can take the appropriate action to manage the situation. If you are genuinely feeling good, then there is no further action required. However, if you are feeling stressed, anxious, depressed, hungry, uncomfortable, tired, or any other unpleasant emotion, you can use this as an opportunity to choose a solution and work with yourself to achieve a better overall state.

Asking yourself how you are doing forces you to take a moment to really consider how you are actually doing. If you find it's difficult to come up with an answer, then simply adjust your questions. Ask: "Hey heart, how are you doing?" and then consider your emotional state. Are you feeling comfortable or uncomfortable? Then, ask "hey mind, how are you doing?" and allow yourself to answer that question. Is your mind at peace, or is something troubling you? Next, ask yourself "hey body, how are you doing?" and consider your body for a moment. Is your body feeling energized and functional, or is there tension or pain being carried somewhere within' you? Finally, ask "hey soul, how are you doing?" and consider that for a moment. Are there any wanted, hopes, dreams or spiritual needs going unmet? Once you get the answer to each question, take a few minutes to generate a solution so that you can resolve the problem. Then, you can take action on the resolution and move forward feeling more whole and at peace with yourself.

Mindful Breathing

Sometimes when we are feeling out of control with our emotions or thoughts the best thing we can do is take a moment and breathe through it. With stress and anxiety especially, the answer isn't always to bring yourself back into the present moment immediately. Instead, you want to take a few minutes to breathe it out. If you are experiencing a heightened level of stress or anxiety, take a few minutes to breathe it out. You will find that you are feeling much better afterwards.

Deep breathing is a great daily exercise, and it is involved in almost all of the other mindfulness practices. If you desire, you can add deep breathing as an activity all on its own. It can help you generate peace and calmness within' your body which provides you with an excellent foundation for practicing mindfulness techniques. If you choose to add it to your daily routine, spend a few minutes before your daily practices working with your breath. You should also follow your daily practices with the breathing technique.

Breathing is simple, we do it every day all day long. Whether we realize it or not, we are breathing. Turning breathing into a mindfulness practice is extremely simple and mainly requires you to bring your awareness to your breath.

You want to start by simply becoming aware of your breath. Don't try and manipulate it or change it in any way. Instead, simple take a moment to notice every time you breathe in and out. Try and become aware over how long each breath lasts and what you feel like as you are breathing. Can you identify where the breath is being stored? Are you breathing into your throat, lungs, or belly? Let yourself become aware over your own breath for about 30 breaths or one minute.

Once you are aware of your natural breath, take a few moments to start adjusting it. Breathe in just a little longer each time, and breathe out just a little longer each time. Continue lengthening the process until each breath feels deep and relaxing. Make sure you are breathing into your diaphragm and not your chest as it will make you feel even more relaxed.

Science shows that when we are stressed our breath shallows and when we are relaxed our breath deepens. As a result, when we control our breath to be deeper and slower, our body will naturally relax with the breath. You can use this as an opportunity to eliminate stress and difficult emotions and welcome relaxation and peace into your life. Use this technique any time you need to draw stress out of your life and infuse it with peace and calmness.

Short mindfulness practices are powerful for helping you cope with day-to-day activities. You can use these practices to establish your beginner-level daily routine. Each one will allow you to begin building the foundation for your overall mindfulness practice and will give you the opportunity to truly start exploring your inner self. Remember, even though mindfulness practices are generally the same from one person to the next, your own journey will differ based on your unique life events and circumstances. Your past, present, and inner being will all shape the way you experience the world around you. As a result, your response to mindfulness practices and to life itself will be unique to you. Try not to judge yourself based on how you deal with things or compare yourself to others based on how they deal with things. This journey is your own and you should take the time to genuinely embrace it and learn as much about yourself as you possibly can.

When you are in the process of moving forward to advanced techniques, don't feel the need to erase the short techniques. While these techniques will alter to become a part of your daily routine, you should continue to keep them in your mindfulness toolbox as remedies for your day-to-day experiences. If you experience discomforts in the office, while driving, at home, in the supermarket, or anywhere else these tools are excellent to help you come back to the present moment and respond in your chosen manner. These tools are excellent for when you need something in a pinch and don't have several minutes to go through an elaborate routine to bring yourself back to the room.

Remember, when the short practices begin to be used as remedies throughout the day you are not using them as an opportunity to repress emotions that you do not want to experience. Rather, you use them to bring yourself back to the room and move your emotions and difficulties to the side until you can face them head on. When you return to your daily routines, be sure to take advantage of the opportunity to bring those emotions back to the surface and work through them efficiently. By bringing them back and working through them properly, you give yourself the ability to truly eliminate them instead of leaving them to build up and become a greater problem later on.

CHAPTER 3

Advanced Practices

While you do not want to rush into the advanced mindfulness practices, eventually you are going to need to venture beyond the short practices. Advanced mindfulness practices give you the opportunity to elaborate on your short practices and establish a more sustainable routine that will enable you to maintain your mindfulness for years to come.

As mentioned in the previous chapter, don't erase the short practices completely. Instead, use them as remedies for day-to-day experiences and bring yourself back to these emotions during the following routines to help you work through them effectively.

You will notice that the advanced practices are actually routines instead of simple practices. That is because routines encourage your mind and body to respond in certain ways. Therefore, having actual routine practices in place means that when you begin the routine your mind will be conditioned to respond to it in the most effective way possible. As a result, you will be able to easily bring yourself into a mindful state and work through anything you need to work through.

The following practices include a morning routine, a night time routine, individual practices you should be using throughout the day, and tips to help you maintain your mindfulness effectively. These are the strategies you will use on a more regular basis to keep your mindfulness practice strong, so take your time and begin to get to know them really well. If you need to, you can adjust some of the practices to suit your needs better.

When you are in the process of transitioning from beginner to advance, you will want to do so slowly. Start by adding a morning routine, then a night time routine. Then, you can start adding the daily practices and utilizing the tips to keep everything flowing smoothly. There is no need to rush into the switch. In fact, the slower you take it, the faster everything will stick and you will be able to comfortably use it for years to come. Remember, take everything at your own pace and be mindful over your own desires and needs. If you need to alter something or switch up the order in which things are done, then it is more effective to do so then it is to avoid it and make the practice uncomfortable for you as a result.

Mindful Morning Routine

In order to truly master your mindfulness practice, you will want to have a regular morning routine in place. Morning routines allow you to start your day out with the right frame of mind in order to tackle the rest of your day from a mindful perspective. Of course, you will still need to check in and refresh that perspective. However, starting your day out right can minimize the number of refreshers you will need throughout the day.

There are a few important elements to a mindful morning routine. The following steps will guide you through the process of an ideal routine. Of course, you can adjust yours to fit your needs better. Remember, we all learn and grow in different ways, so feel free to make any adjustments you need in order to achieve the maximum benefit from your own practice.

First Breaths

When you first wake in the morning, you may feel compelled to jump out of bed and head to the bathroom. Although it is satisfying to relieve yourself after a long night's sleep, it can also have you feeling a little rattled first thing in the morning. Instead of leaping out of bed, try starting your first mindful practice of the day.

Your first breaths of the day should be wholesome and relaxing. Take a few moments to take three deep, refreshing breaths. Ultimately, you want to hold fast to those relaxing breaths we take as we are asleep. Allow your body to breathe naturally, but also allow for it to stay in a relaxed state. Don't manipulate the breath to become shallow or fast by feeling a rush to get up. There is no need to prolong this practice. Simply allow yourself to become mindful over your breath for the first three breaths of your morning. When you are done, you can rise from bed and prepare yourself for the rest of your day. Make sure you relieve yourself, and then have a nice large glass of cool water before moving on to the rest of the mindfulness routine.

Gratitude

When you express gratitude first thing in the morning, you set the tone for the rest of the day. Your mindset will be calm and pure, and you will naturally start looking for the wonderful aspects of your day. Gratitude practices are taught in virtually every mindfulness lesson because they have such a powerful impact on the way you live your life. It can certainly pay off to listen to the advice and start implementing your own gratitude practice throughout the day.

There are many ways that you can implement a gratitude practice into your life. Depending on what feels comfortable for you, you may wish to say it out loud, think it quietly in your mind, or write it down in a journal. It does not matter what way you choose, as long as it feels satisfying to you.

Before you start expressing gratitude, take a few moments to take a deep breath. Try and challenge yourself to dig deeper. Of course, expressing gratitude for anything is important, but often we get caught up in expressing it for obvious things: cars, money, friends, luxuries, and more. While you should certainly express gratitude for these things, try and challenge yourself to pick five things that you may not normally think about. For example, the pen you are writing with, the sun visor in your car, the bulb in your lamp, so on and so forth. When you start to look more closely at what you have, you learn to appreciate things more deeply. Often we become oblivious to just how much we have in life. Mindfulness practices such as this allow you to learn how you can look more critically at the world around you and truly see exactly what you have and offer appreciation for it.

Mindful Meditation

Each morning routine should have some form of mindfulness meditation involved. How long you choose to meditate for is unique to you, but the average recommended time is between 5 and 15 minutes. Anything longer than 15 minutes is not entirely necessary.

In order to practice your mindful meditation in the morning, start by sitting in a comfortable position and closing your eyes. Then, you can start focusing on your breath. There is no need to manipulate or control your breath, simply focus on it. Once you are focused on your breath, hold your focus there for a while. If you notice that your attention is wandering, take a moment and gently guide it back to your breath. It is natural for your attention to wander, especially so early in the morning. Never punish yourself for this. Instead, simply acknowledge what has happened and draw your awareness back.

Mindful meditation is a powerful practice that can help bring you into the present moment in a gentle way. You should include meditation in your mindfulness morning routine even if you choose to adjust this routine in any way. If you struggle to gauge the amount of time that you have been meditating for, set an alarm on your phone for 5 to 15 minutes from the moment you start. Then, you can simply focus on your breath and trust that you will know when to stop when the alarm rings.

Body Scan

Conducting a body scan first thing in the morning is important. After a long night of sleep we can often wake up with residual tension.  They may be tensions that we hold on to from sleep, or they may be tensions that we hold on to from the day before. Regardless of where they come from, taking a moment to identify them and work through them can help eliminate them as you carry on to tackle the rest of your day.

If you desire, you can move directly from your meditation into your body scan. Alternatively, you may wish to adjust yourself and then get comfortable again for the body scan. That is entirely up to you.

To start your body scan you want to be relaxed and have your eyes closed. Ideally you should be sitting or lying down in a position that is open and loose. You do not want to be clenching anything, tucking anything in, or otherwise creating your own bodily discomforts. The more relaxed and loosened your body is, the better. Once you are relaxed, take a moment to start mindfully scanning through your body parts. Start with the crown of your head, down your forehead and the back of your skull, and through the middle. Take a moment to notice your ears, eyes, and nose. Then, move down to the cheeks, mouth, and jaw. If you notice any tension or discomfort in these areas, take a few moments to focus upon that area and send it love. See if you can discover anything about this area and find out why there is discomfort being held there. If you can find out why, take a mental note so that you can resolve this issue going forward. For example, if your jaw is tense from stress at work, your resolve may be to reduce the stress you experience at work by increasing your mindfulness practice and allowing yourself to release emotions at the end of the day.

After scanning your head, move down to your neck and shoulders. Then, move down your arms into your biceps and triceps, down through your elbows and into your forearms. Finally, scan your wrists, palms, and fingers all the way to the tips. Again, if you notice any discomfort in any of these areas, take a few moments to send love to it and see if you can discover what the issue appears to be.

Next, you want to scan your chest, down through your torso and into your waist. Take some time noticing your pelvic bone and your hips, then move down through your glutes and into your thighs. Then, you can scan down to your knees, through your calves, and into your ankles and feet. End your scan by moving your awareness all the way through your toes. As you may suspect, if you notice any tension or discomfort in these areas take some time to send love and awareness to the area and do your best to identify the root cause of the problem.

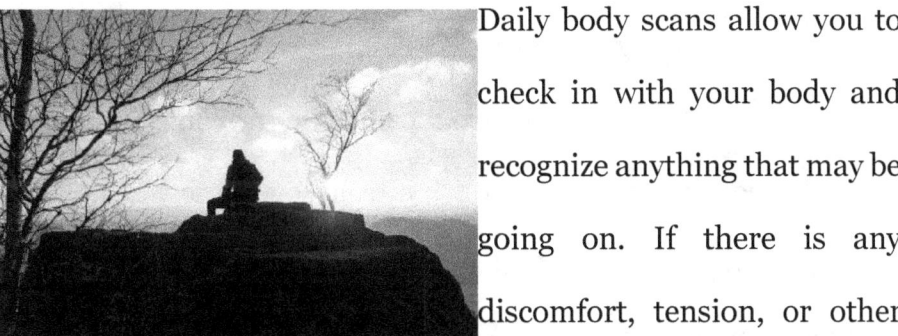

Daily body scans allow you to check in with your body and recognize anything that may be going on. If there is any discomfort, tension, or other unwelcomed feelings you want to take the time to become aware of these things. When you do, you give yourself the ability to recognize what your body needs and give it what it is asking for. If you do not respect your body when it asks for what it needs, the problem will grow until the point where it is unavoidable. It is best to get in control of everything ahead of time rather than waiting for it to get worse and then wishing you had dealt with it sooner. As a result of taking care of your body in this way, you will notice that it starts to feel healthier and better overall. Because of this, you will feel a greater sense of peace and happiness because you will not be physically uncomfortable or at dis-ease.

Check In

After a thorough body scan it is a great time to check in with your emotional self. Take this opportunity to ask yourself how you are feeling. Then, take a moment to notice what answers come up for you.

When you are doing this practice, it is a good idea to have your journal handy. Writing down what comes up for you can help you work through it. You might notice a trend over a few days if you have an issue that is particularly difficult for you. Additionally, writing it down can give you a different perspective on the situation which can assist you with working through it.

Your check in process doesn't have to take long. Simply ask yourself how you are doing and then allow yourself to honestly answer the question. Some days you might find that you are doing well, others you might find that you are struggling with a particular set of emotions. Either way, it is important to know so that you can keep in touch with your emotional body and nurture it the same way you would want to nurture your physical body if anything were to be wrong with it.

Mindful Breathing

Finally, you want to wrap up your morning routine with a mindful breathing practice. Once again, take a few moments to bring your awareness to your breath. This time you are going to want to be mindful of ten full breaths. There is no need to manipulate these breaths to be longer or shorter, deeper or more shallow. You can simply become aware of how your body is naturally breathing in this very moment.

Once you have completed your ten breaths, you are done your morning routine! The entire process should take you no longer than about half an hour, depending on how long you choose to take in order to complete each practice. After completing a powerful morning routine, you will likely feel a lot better about starting your entire day. Often times we take minimum care of our bodies in the morning. We relieve ourselves, slam a glass of water, eat some breakfast, jump in the shower, dress ourselves and then run out the door. When we rush through the motions this way and fail to actually take care of our body the way it needs to be cared for, we set ourselves up for failure. A body that is being ignored is a body that does not perform at its peak function. If your body is failing to perform at its peak function, it is because you are not nurturing it the way it needs to be. Your body will always tell you what it needs, all you need to do is take a moment to turn into the silence and listen. When you do this, you give yourself the opportunity to care for yourself in the best way possible and as a result your body will serve you to its highest ability.

Mindful Night Time Routine

In addition to a powerful mindful morning routine, you need to have a powerful mindful night time routine as well. The night time routine will allow you to shed the stress of the day and truly prepare yourself for bed time so that you can have a restful sleep that will provide you with the ability to have a wonderful morning.

Most people report that their largest concern is fatigue and a lack of sleep. Many times, even if you are getting the appropriate hours of sleep per night, your sleep is not high quality because you are not relieving yourself from stress and tension before bed. As a result, you suffer from low sleep quality because your body simply cannot rest deeply enough. Your physical, psychological and emotional bodies will all suffer from your lack of attention, which can be extremely difficult to endure especially after a prolonged period of time.

The best night time routine is simple, relaxing, and takes very little time. This routine takes about 20-30 minutes for you to complete and it ends with you getting into your bed. Because of that, you want to make this the last thing you do before you sleep. If you do this too early in the night you may open yourself up to receive more stress and tension before bed which will ultimately negate from the benefit of this practice.

Mindful Breathing and Grounding

The first thing you want to do when you are starting your night time routine is practice mindful breathing and ground yourself. Start with the breathing. You can do this by taking a few deep breaths and drawing your awareness into each breath. Once your attention is rested upon your breath, take about 10 more breaths. Notice the way each breath feels. Take some time to recognize which areas of your body are affected by the breath. You can also become aware of what your natural breathing is like in that moment, and notice if it changes over the course of the ten breaths. Once you are in total awareness of your breath, shift your focus to the floor beneath your feet. Become aware of how it supports your feet no matter where you are. At any time in your life you can rest your feet firmly on the floor and it will support you no matter where you are, what you are doing, or how you are feeling. Next, bring your attention to the surface that your body is rested upon. Notice how your body feels as it settles into the support.

Finally, start looking at the room around you. Notice anything that stands out for you. If you see anything new, take some time to notice that. If there are any sounds that are standing out to you, really become aware about those as well. Take a few seconds to notice what they are and how they affect the way you feel and think about the present moment.

After you are completely grounded, move into a body scan.

Body Scan

As with all of the previous body scans, this body scan is going to enable you to look through your entire body and notice anywhere that may be holding tension or discomfort. Doing this after you are grounded will ensure that you do not spend this time fixated on other concerns from your daily experiences. You can do this scan in your bed so that you are ready for sleep afterward.

This time your body scan is going to be slightly different. You are going to relax and imagine as though there is a gold light moving through your body. As the light fills more of you up any tension, stress, negativity or discomfort will be displaced until finally it is pushed out of your body completely.

Start by relaxing and imagining that there is a golden light above your head. As you notice it, notice that it starts slowly moving towards the crown of your head. Already, you can feel yourself relaxing as it nears your body. Once it penetrates the crown of your head, imagine it moving down through your entire skull and face, washing through to your neck and shoulders. Any tension that may be built up in your head or jaw is being pushed out of place with the light as it moves down through your neck and shoulders, then all the way down your arms. If there is any tension in your arms, imagine it is being pushed out of the end of your fingertips until there is none left and both of your arms are completely filled with the golden light.

Return your awareness back to your chest and picture the light pushing down through your chest. It moves down through your abdomen towards your hips, pressing everything down your body. Then it moves through your glutes, thighs, knees and calves. Finally, it moves through your ankles and feet, pushing any remaining discomfort, stress, negativity or tension out through the bottoms of your feet.

Once you are done the scan, take a few moments to really picture your body glowing with this golden light. Every ounce of tension and discomfort has been removed from your body and all that remains is the beautiful golden healing energy that allows you to feel deeply relaxed and comfortable in the moment. Any tension that was not directly dealt with can be focused on in your morning routine. Now is not the time to work through the tensions, but rather to melt them away so that you can relax. They can be dealt with at a later time.

Instead of coming out of this meditative state, simply move on to the mindful meditation practice.

Mindful Meditation

Now that you are already relaxed from your body scan, it is a great time to move on to your mindful meditation. After you are done imagining the golden light, take a few moments to bring your awareness to your breath. Notice how deep or shallow it is, how frequently you are breathing, and what parts of your body are being affected by the breath.

This time, there is no need to set an alarm as you are simply going to meditate until right before you fall asleep. Make sure you don't meditate until you pass out because this can lead to the unwanted habit of you falling asleep every time you try to meditate, rather than you actually effectively meditating.

Acknowledge the breath for as long as you comfortably can. At night, we have a tendency to let our minds wander. If you notice this is happening, bring your attention back to your breath. Do not punish yourself for this, rather gently bring back your attention. Eventually, it will be significantly easier for you to stay entirely focused on the meditation process. Practice your meditation until you are just about to pass out.

One Last Stretch

Before you are about to fall asleep and after you finish your meditation, take a moment to stretch yourself out one last time. Start with your feet and toes, stretch them out completely and then tighten them up. Release your tension and let your feet relax completely. Next, stretch out your legs and then clench them. After a moment, release the clench and let them relax completely. Now you want to do this same patter for your glutes, your abdomen, your hands, your arms, your chest, and your shoulders. Finally, do it for your neck, jaw, and face. When you are done, your entire body should feel completely relaxed.

Final Breaths

Just before you pass out, take three mindful breaths. Notice how your entire body feels, notice where your breath is at, and notice what it feels like to be breathing in that pattern. When you are done, you can close your eyes and fall asleep.

Having a night time routine like this can teach you to release the tension from the day and enter a peaceful state of mind before bed. It gives you the opportunity to relax entirely so that when you rest you have a deep sleep. People who do not mindfully release their daily tension often go to bed stressed out and as a result they have poor sleep quality. They end up living in a constant state of fatigue because they are not sleeping well, even if they are sleeping an adequate number of hours per night. Many other ailments can arise from poor sleep quality, which you do not want to experience. Having this routine in place, or a similar routine, will allow you to get a high quality rest so that you are able to feel alert and awake the next day.

Every Day Mindfulness

In addition to morning and night time routines, you want to have practices you use throughout the day as well. In the "simple practices" chapter, you were taught a variety of powerful mini-strategies that enable you to maintain control over your mindfulness practice throughout the day. You should continue using those strategies in order to maintain your day-to-day mindfulness practice.

In case you have forgotten which practices those were, they included:

- Grounding Technique
- Short Body Scan
- How Are You Doing?
- Mindful Breathing

In addition to these simple practices, there are a few other areas in which you can infuse your life with mindfulness. They include:

Eating

When you are eating, make sure you are taking some time to truly absorb the experience of your meal. Chew slowly, really notice each flavor in your meal, and take your time in between bites. When you feel satisfied, do not force yourself to eat more. Do not rush yourself, and do not treat it as a chore. Instead, truly experience the process. You will likely learn a lot about yourself and your preferences during this process.

Often, we treat eating like a chore. We go to drive-thru restaurants or we eat convenience meals and we leave out the experience of cooking and preparing our meal. We don't get the experience of plating it and truly looking at it before we eat it because we are in such a rush to eat it as quickly as possible and resume our busy lifestyles. Instead of doing this, make the entire process a mindfulness practice. Take your time when you are preparing the meal, plate it carefully in a way that looks attractive to you, and take your time eating it. Your health will improve significantly as well, as you will not be over eating or indulging in unhealthy food choices anymore.

Listening

It is common that we listen only for the purpose of responding. We never truly hear everything the other person is saying, rather we hear enough to formulate a response and then we stop listening as deeply. Doing this is ineffective as it can lead to misunderstandings and you not absorbing all of the information from the conversation. Instead of listening merely to respond, listen simply to listen. Respond afterwards, when you have received all of the information and have had a moment to thoughtfully think it over.

Listen to each word the person says, and pay attention to their body language as well. Notice what signs they are giving you based on their facial expressions and hand gestures, as well as their posture. Take some time to acknowledge the feelings they are putting into the conversation. When you listen this way, you absorb the entire message that is being offered by the speaker. Then, you can respond in a manner that is truly productive to the conversation. Additionally, you can learn a great deal of knowledge this way.

Speaking and Thinking

The way we speak and think is often uncensored. Many times, we think and say things that are toxic to ourselves or the world around us. We think or speak judgmentally and tear down others and ourselves along the way. As a result, we infuse our lives with a great deal of negativity because we fail to think before we speak.

Instead of simply saying or thinking the first thing that comes to your mind, take a moment to become aware of the thought. Notice what the tone is. Is it judgmental, or is it positive? Will it hurt if it is thought or spoken? Or can it add genuine value?

Thoughts that are deemed negative, hurtful, or otherwise unproductive should be mindfully released in favor of ones that are positive and productive. This way, you are only using your mind power and words to add positivity to the world.

Mindfulness Maintenance Tips

Practicing mindfulness may be difficult for some people. The following is a variety of tips that can help you add depth to your practice and gain the most out of it.

Triggers

Having "triggers" that remind you to check in with yourself is a great way to start practicing mindfulness throughout the day. When you are learning to implement mindfulness into your daily activities it can be difficult, especially never having done it before. Triggers can be any number of things that, when you notice them, you are triggered to remember that you want to practice mindfulness in that moment. So, imagine your trigger was a clock. Any time you saw a clock you would be triggered to ask "how am I doing?" and then choose a solution based on the answer. Over time you will become so used to asking yourself how you are doing that it will come naturally, whether you see the trigger or not. You will also develop a sense of awareness about yourself that will enable you to know exactly what you need in order to feel better in moments of discomfort which will allow you to promptly resolve any issues that arise.

Triggers can be virtually anything. You may choose a clock, a pen, a specific car, a certain number, a certain word, or anything else. Whatever you choose is completely up to you. Choose something that you will see on a regular basis and then consciously decide that any time you see that item you will remember to ask yourself how you are doing.

At first, you may forget to act on the trigger. However, you will have some form of reaction to the trigger simply because your mind will remember "hey, there was something about clocks that I was supposed to remember". That simple reaction is a great start. Quickly, you will know exactly what the clock is meant to trigger and you will remember to ask the question. It takes time, so be patient with yourself and give it time to sink in.

Journaling

Journaling is a wonderful tool to add to your mindfulness practice. While it may not be ideal to journal everything throughout the entire day, using journaling for larger practices (such as your morning and night time routines) is a great idea.

Your journal can serve you in many ways. First, you can use your journal to write down any experiences that you may be having or any responses you have to certain questions. You can also use it to express gratitude for things in your life. As you are writing all of this down, you are also tracking all of your growth in your mindfulness practice. Any time you want, you can flip back through your pages and notice just how far you have come since you started. It is a good idea to keep a pen and your journal handy near the spot where you generally practice your morning and night time routines. That way, you can journal on a regular basis and keep track of everything that comes up for you.

Setting Alarms

If triggers aren't enough or you are struggling to remember the purpose of the trigger, you might consider using alarms as well. In your phone, you can set an alarm for every hour that alerts you asking "How are you doing?" That way, you are prompted to check in with yourself on an hourly basis.

Over time, the alarm will serve you in two ways. First, it will teach you to practice mindfulness every hour so that you can stay in touch with yourself and how you are doing. Second, it will turn your phone notifications into a trigger. You will come to expect that notifications on your phone mean that you are being reminded to check in with yourself, therefore any notification you get will remind you to ask yourself how you are doing. It's a wonderful win-win situation!

Making it Personal

The final most important thing you should do when you are developing your mindfulness practice is to make it personal. A mindfulness practice that is copied directly from a book or a guide is one that will likely not mirror exactly what you need. In the beginning, following the guide exactly is a great idea. Over time, however, you will likely identify areas that could serve you better if they were adjusted. Feel confident that if you make these adjustments, your mindfulness practice will serve you even better.

The practice of mindfulness is a highly personal one. It is a journey of your inner self, one that only you can experience. You may be able to share the story with others, but only you can have the true experience yourself. Because of that, only you know exactly what you need from your experience in order for it to serve your highest good. When you adjust your mindfulness practices to reflect these needs, you strengthen it and empower it to serve you in a way that will keep your practice incredibly successful and allow you to master your own mindfulness.

Advancing your mindfulness practice is important. Although you may settle into a sort of routine with your practice, you will likely notice that even the routine is adjusted several times over throughout your life. Your needs and present states of being are constantly changing and therefore your mindfulness practice will constantly change as well. The practices in this section are for you to learn how to transition from a beginner's level to an advanced level of mindfulness practice. From here, it is up to you to continue developing your practice and evolving it into what it needs to be in order to serve your highest good. If you ever feel stuck or as though your practice is fading, return to this chapter and start following it exactly once again. Doing this will refresh your mind and bring you back into the center of your practice, allowing you to continue evolving it for your greater good.

CHAPTER 4

Digging Deeper

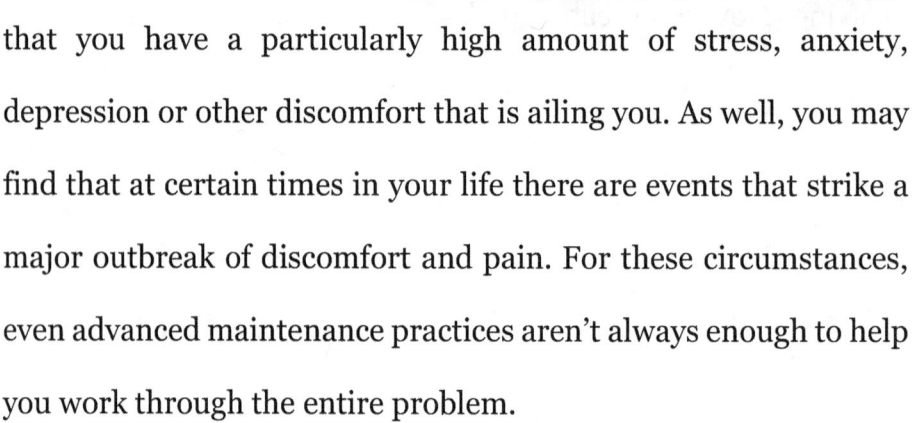

Daily practices and maintenance routines are important, but they cannot always resolve large issues. When you are new to mindfulness, you may find that you have a particularly high amount of stress, anxiety, depression or other discomfort that is ailing you. As well, you may find that at certain times in your life there are events that strike a major outbreak of discomfort and pain. For these circumstances, even advanced maintenance practices aren't always enough to help you work through the entire problem.

For this purpose, you are going to explore the digging deeper section. You will be guided through the process of getting to the source of the problem and then eliminating it entirely. In doing so, you will effectively release unwanted discomfort without repressing it in a way that leads to greater discomfort. Ultimately, it is one of the healthiest ways for you to work through anything that ails you. Of course, if you are struggling significantly you should seek professional assistance so that you can resolve anything you may be suffering with. Mindfulness is merely a tool and not a total healing treatment. If you are having great difficulty getting through a hard time, it is highly recommended that you allow a professional to assist you through and use mindfulness as an additional tool for the process.

Getting to the Root Cause

The first part of the process is getting to the root cause of the deep-set discomfort. Depending on what it is, you may not actually know exactly what event caused you to get the discomfort. So, if you can't identify the exact event you at least want to identify the exact emotion. For example, stress may actually be grief, anger, or feeling as though you have not spoken your truth. The clearer you get about what the actual problem is, the more effective you will be in dealing with it.

You can get to the root of these emotions and discomforts by practicing a mindfulness meditation that allows you to truly explore the feeling itself. In doing so, you will learn a great deal about the discomfort and why it exists in the first place. For this meditation, you will want to be in a calm space, and you may wish to have music on. You will then want to be sitting or lying down in a comfortable position that will allow you to meditate without falling asleep.

Start by bringing your awareness to your breath and your body. For now, put the discomfort out of your mind completely. You want to bring your mind into a meditative state that will allow you to tune into your body and become totally aware of the discomfort you are experiencing. To do this, focus on your breath for about 20-30 breaths. When you start to feel relaxed, that is when you want to stop counting and simply maintain your focus on your breath. Take stress and anticipation away and simply spend a few moments appreciating your breath and body.

Once you are completely relaxed, you can start to focus in on the areas that you are feeling the tension or discomfort. Start with just one area. Don't try and manipulate the discomfort in any way, simply bring your awareness to the discomfort. Notice where it is, what it is affecting, and how much it is affecting you. Does the pain feel significant, or small but persistent? At this time, you simply want to identify all of the feelings you are having around the discomfort. If you can, ask the discomfort where it has come from and see if any answers come up for you. Try and understand the discomfort itself and where you have acquired it from.

Once you are more aware about the discomfort itself, how it's affecting you and where it might be coming from, you can simply start to send love to it. The purpose of getting to the root cause is not to alter the discomfort, but rather to understand it more. You are validating the discomfort, becoming aware of its presence and purpose. Following your mindfulness meditation around the discomfort, you can use the root cause as your basis for making necessary changes in your life to prevent it from getting worse and reduce the discomfort as it is. These changes vary greatly. You may simply need to sleep more at night to reduce headaches from tiredness, or you may need to nurture yourself more as you work to reduce heartache from grief. The process does not come from directly eliminating the source but rather understanding it and giving yourself the space to properly work through it so that you can move past it.

It is vital that you remember that the purpose is never to completely distinguish discomfort or unwanted emotions by repressing them or "putting them aside". Instead, you want to get to the root source and genuinely work through it. That way the ailment is completely resolved and you can move forward to carry on with your life, knowing you are at peace with the issue itself.

During your meditation where you are beginning to address the root cause, you may wish to spend a significant amount of time sending love to the discomfort. In doing so, you are validating the emotion and feeling and giving yourself the space to work through what you need to work through in order to move past the discomfort.

Addressing Painful Emotions

There are many times in life where we may encounter painful emotions. Often times we naturally want to repress these emotions because facing them can be extremely difficult. Feeling the painful emotions as they are can feel even more painful, so it can be easy to want to avoid them. When you avoid them, however, you make the pain worse. You end up feeling the pain significantly more in the long run, as well as many other symptoms that arise as a result of this pain being repressed for so long. The better thing to do is to mindfully work through the emotions.

There are many ways that you can mindfully work through emotions, but it is important to note that every way will require you to take the time to actually work through the emotions. The first part of working through difficult emotions is identifying exactly what they are. It can take some time, but you need to really recognize what you are experiencing. For example, are you stressed because of work, or are you experiencing residual anger from a previous argument and therefore taking the emotional burden to work, thus causing your work to be stressful? Identifying exactly what is causing the difficult emotions is what will allow you to genuinely work through them. While you will want to work through all of the symptoms as well, it is important that you start with the primary purpose.

At first, you may not know what the primary reason is. If that is the case, start with what you think is the primary reason. Through that work, you will likely discover what the actual purpose of the difficult emotions are. With the emotions you are working through, you will want to follow these steps in order to effectively work through them.

The first thing you want to do is to really get clear on what the emotion is and where it came from. It can be beneficial to journal through this process. Start by writing down what you are feeling and why you think you are feeling it. From there, continue writing about what emotions you are feeling and any symptoms you are experiencing as a result. Don't think about what you are writing, simply continue writing about everything that comes into your mind. You will likely discover many more emotions or feelings through this writing exercise that will be brought to light when you stop thinking and start exploring what you are feeling inside.

After you have done this writing exercise, you can start identifying what the primary emotions and symptoms are that you are experiencing. Then, you should give yourself space to work through them. This part of the process may look different for everyone. Depending on what emotion you are experiencing, you may have a different way that you need to work through it. For example, if you are feeling grief you may wish to cry. If you are feeling anger, you may wish to go for a jog or punch a punching bag to release your energy. Depending on what you are feeling, you will want to experience it.

It is important that you work through the emotions in a way that feels right to you. You will likely already have an idea of what you need to do in order to work through your emotions. Something will likely have been lingering in your mind, encouraging you to work through the emotions in a specific way. If you have been having these encouraging feelings, you should take the time to explore them and see how the results make you feel.

It is important that you understand the purpose of emotions. Being mindful about the reason why we experience emotions can allow you to mindfully approach your emotions and reduce your tendency to push them down.

Emotions are feelings that we experience as a result of our life events. We experience many emotions on a day-to-day basis, varying in degrees. The emotions can be pleasurable, or they can be uncomfortable. They can change rapidly, and they can be hard to ignore. The reason behind this is because emotions virtually always bring about a lesson, breakthrough, or deeper understanding of our inner self.

When an emotion is being experienced to serve a lesson, there is only one way that you can actually solve the emotion. That is, you must go through the lesson. The more you avoid learning the lesson, the greater the emotion will become until you absolutely must face it. Alternatively, you may wind up with significant levels of stress, anxiety, depression, or other unwanted emotions. Lessons are generally hard and can push us to step outside of our comfort zone. For example, you may have to speak up for yourself or initiate a confrontation that is outside of what you would typically be comfortable doing. The process of actually speaking up or initiating the confrontation may be extremely difficult but once you complete the task there will be a rewarding experience at the end. This "feel good" experience that you have when you have done something difficult like this is the result of successfully navigating your way through a life lesson.

Breakthroughs are generally what we experience when we have been faced with a life lesson that we have regularly ignored or avoided. When we ignore or avoid life lessons, we no longer experience a simple passing through when we accomplish the lesson. Instead, we often experience what is known as a breakthrough. This means that when you get through to the other side, a large majority of your life will shift for the better. Parts of your life that you have been shrinking and neglecting in order to avoid the lesson will be a part of your breakthrough and you will have a total transformation in your life and psyche as a result.

When we experience deep emotions that are connected to understanding ourselves better, generally the only thing we need to do is experience the emotion. We will learn a great deal about ourselves as a result. You may learn how you naturally respond to various emotions, you may learn about what causes you to experience these emotions, or you may learn about any other number of things. The only way to explore this deeper version of yourself is to actually experience the emotions.

Regardless of why you are experiencing emotions in your life, you need to work through them. The best way is to write down the emotion and let yourself free write as you further explore the emotion. Once you have explored it this way, you can then allow yourself some space and freedom to actually feel your way through the emotion.

The Power of Releasing

Learning to release things is important. Many times you may find that you have worked through emotions but due to poor coping skills you wind up replaying the emotions over and over in your mind. Often this means that you haven't fully worked through the emotion, but other times it can be because you fail to release things after you are done working through them. Effectively releasing things when you are done working through them is an important way to put them in the past and let them go.

The best way that you can release something is to meditate and consciously let it go. Start by breathing deeply and relaxing yourself until you are in a meditative state. Then, you can draw your awareness into your mind's eye. Imagine as though you are walking down a flight of stairs. Take them one stair at a time, genuinely experiencing each stair as you move. Once you get to the bottom, you will notice that there is a door there. You can enter the door and walk through. Behind the door there will be a large, warm, comfy chair that is waiting for you. When you see the chair, you can sit in it and begin to relax.

After you are relaxed in the chair, you can start imagining anything that is causing you severe discomfort. Picture a thought bubble that rises above your head and fill the bubble with everything that ails you. Anything that is lingering and causing you residual pain should be put into this bubble so that you can let it go.

Once you are done putting all of the thoughts and images into the bubble, imagine that the dots connecting the bubble to your head fade away. Then, you can take a deep breath and blow at the bubble. Continue blowing it, as you blow it away from you. Eventually, it will get so far that it starts to fade away and you can no longer see it. Soon, it will completely fade and will be nothing but a distant, neutralized memory.

When you can no longer see the bubble, take a few moments to breathe deeply. Imagine that you are already living life free of any of the residual pain you were experiencing. Notice how much more free you feel when you are no longer a victim of the painful remnants of emotions. Take some time to say to yourself "I am free". Preferably, say it at least three times over. When you are done, smile and take a few more deep breaths. Then, you can stand up from the chair, exit the room and close the door firmly behind you. Walk one by one up each stair until you are at the top of the stairs. Then, you can take a few more deep breaths and open your eyes and return to the actual room that surrounds you. When you are ready, you can stretch out your limbs and prepare yourself to return to your daily life.

Releasing techniques are important because they can help eliminate emotional build up. Sometimes you will want to use releasing techniques in addition to addressing painful emotions

because there is so much to work through. You won't always be able to work through everything in one or two sessions. Sometimes you will have to work through things a few times until you completely address all of the unwanted feelings and release everything.

If you are working through addressing painful emotions, you should always practice some form of release afterward. Releasing after each session is a way of gaining closure from the session. It essentially seals the deal. You might think of the process of addressing painful emotions as being the bleeding of a wound and then the process of releasing being your wound scabbing over. The healing process deepens when you properly release all of the residual build up around it.

Alternatively, some days you may experience a significant amount of negative energies. Stress may build up and as a result the negativity of your daily environment may affect you more than normal. If this happens, you will want to practice releasing as well. In this case, you are simply releasing unwanted energies. This is different from ignoring emotions as in this instance there are generally no real emotions to be released. Instead, you are simply releasing the build up after a particularly difficult day.

Releasing is a powerful technique that can be done in many ways. When you look around you may discover that there are hundreds, if not thousands of methods for you to release unwanted energies and emotions after you are done working through them. Some may give you the illusion that if you use the technique you can release unwanted emotions before you have effectively worked through them. Please take the time to note that this is untrue and is never possible. Any time you attempt to release unwanted emotions before working through them, you are merely suppressing them to be dealt with at a later time. There is virtually no way to run away from your emotions. You must deal with them at one time or another. The longer you wait, the harder it will be for you to work through it.

When Your Practice Fades

There comes a time in every mindfulness practitioner's life where their practice fades. This is completely natural. When you are busy in life, have a lot going on, or are struggling with difficult emotions or circumstances, it can be easy to negate away from your mindfulness practice. Sometimes you might think you will come back to it shortly, other times your mindfulness practice might appear as though it is the source of your pain. The specific reason as to why your practice has faded will determine how you can address the situation.

If your practice has faded because of a busy schedule or a lack of commitment, the best thing you can do is start at the beginning again. Head back to the "short strategies" section of this book and start practicing smaller sessions on a daily basis. Build yourself back up to the advanced strategy and then carry on as you were. You might find that you have to do this many times throughout your life as you may become busy and experience changes to your schedule that bump you off of your course. Simply restart and carry on and you will have effectively addressed this situation.

If your practice is fading because it no longer serves you in the way you need, you should spend some time addressing this issue. Notice where the practice was no longer serving you and adjust it so that it can begin to fulfill your needs once again. Occasionally we outgrow our mindfulness practices and if we don't adjust our practice we will simply discontinue it because we no longer feel we are gaining value from it. Never feel as though you need to stick to a specific routine or strategy in order to maintain your mindfulness practice. As you grow, you will likely feel natural pulls to adjust or alter it in certain ways. When you experience this, the best thing you can do is appreciate the tugs and follow them. More often than not, your intuition will be able to guide you in the way that will fill your needs the best.

Another thing that commonly draws people away from mindfulness practices is the difficult times. If you are experiencing difficult emotions, you may no longer want to practice your

mindfulness techniques. Because mindfulness encourages you to face the difficulty, it can be easy to want to avoid it so that you don't have to feel the discomfort. If you have been avoiding your practice for this reason, it is extremely important that you don't hold yourself in contempt for it. There is no reason to feel as though you are in need of being punished because you are struggling to face a difficult emotion. Instead, gently guide yourself back into your mindfulness practice. You should start at the beginning by reintroducing the easier strategies into your practice again. As well, when you are ready, you will want to work through the strategies from this chapter. Getting to the root cause, addressing painful emotions and learning to release will all help you effectively work through the process of dealing with the emotions you have been struggling with and moving forward with your life and mindfulness practice. The more you are open to growth and change in your life, the more you will experience.

When your mindfulness practice begins to fade, it is always important that you accept that there is a natural ebb and flow to the practice. You won't always feel as though you are as committed as you once were. Sometimes you will feel more dedicated, other times you will feel less dedicated. Sometimes you may even forget to practice for several days at a time. There is no reason to feel guilty or shameful about these experiences. Instead, recognize that a true mindfulness practice is fluid and the way you feel and the way you work with it will vary from day to day. Many circumstances and factors go into the development of a mindfulness practice, you will simply need to take your time and be patient.

Something worth realizing is that when your mindfulness practices fades, this is generally a powerful opportunity for you to learn more about yourself. When you learn about why it has faded, you can explore that further and develop a greater sense of understanding as to why that was your response and what you can do about it that will genuinely work for you. The more you learn about yourself, the better. After all, that is what mindfulness is all about!

In your mindfulness journey, there will be times when the simple day-to-day maintenance is not enough. You will need to invest some more energy and focus into the development of your practice sometimes. When you are having particularly difficult emotions, are carrying around a large amount of stress, anxiety or depression, or when you are noticing your practice is not as strong as it once was, you will need to implement larger strategies.

These strategies are not ones that need to be used in your daily routine. However, you can and should use them as often as you need to in order to gain the appropriate benefits from them. If you are experiencing particularly large emotions that are difficult for you, it may take several days, weeks, or even months to work through those emotions. Take as long as you need and be gentle with yourself. When you are done, you will return to a place where you can manage your mindfulness with simpler daily routines. Take it easy and always have patience with yourself. The more gentle you are, the quicker you will adapt to your mindfulness practice and gain the benefits from it.

CONCLUSION

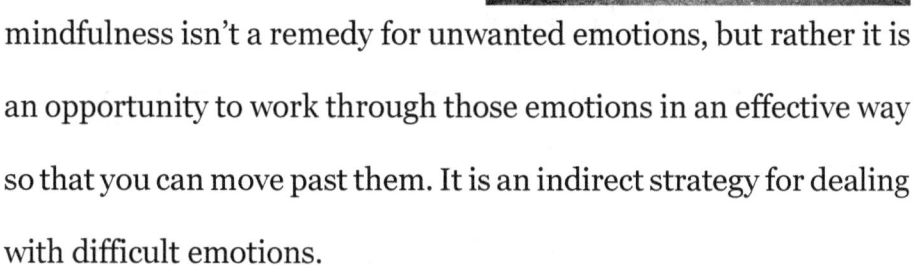

Mindfulness is a powerful practice for helping you eliminate stress, anxiety, depression, and other uncomfortable emotions. It is important to always recognize that mindfulness isn't a remedy for unwanted emotions, but rather it is an opportunity to work through those emotions in an effective way so that you can move past them. It is an indirect strategy for dealing with difficult emotions.

In your own mindfulness practice, you will be encouraged to learn more about yourself. The greater self-awareness you have, the more you will know exactly what you need in order to work through difficult emotions. It may not make it easier for you to work through them, however it will make you more aware as to how you will feel as you do. Ultimately, mindfulness is an exploration of your inner self that leads to a place where you can consciously work together with your emotions to generate a life of peace and happiness.

I hope this book was able to teach you several effective strategies for developing your own mindfulness practice. It is important to start by working up your short strategies and becoming used to them. While you may feel inclined to jump straight into a more advanced practice, the reality is that this is not beneficial. Working in this way can result in you getting in over your head and feeling overwhelmed, thus abandoning your practice and feeling reluctant to start over again. Start small, gain momentum and confidence, and then work your way up. Remember, if you struggle to maintain your practice, simply start over again and take it easy. If you are dealing with intense or difficult emotions, be sure to give yourself the opportunity to address them properly and then release them properly as well.

The next step is for you to start practicing the short strategies in your daily routine. Start small and master this stage first. Once you feel extremely confident in this level, you can move forward to start transitioning into the more advanced practice. Again, when you are transitioning you should still start small. Take it easy with the transition and make sure that you are only adding one part of the advanced strategy at a time. As you feel more confident in each part of the strategy, you can transition more and more until you have fully embraced the advanced level. Then, you can work on maintaining your mindfulness practice and evolving it in the way that feels best for you.

Lastly, if you enjoyed this book I ask that you please take the time to rate it on Amazon Kindle. Your honest review would be greatly appreciated.

Thank you!

STRESS MANAGEMENT FOR BEGINNERS

Guided Meditation Techniques to Reduce Stress, Increase Happiness, and Improve your Health, Body & Mind

Sarah Rowland

INTRODUCTION

Congratulations on downloading this book and thank you for doing so.

The following chapters will discuss causes of stress and several ways to manage and eliminate stressors in your life.

There are plenty of books on this subject on the market, thanks again for choosing this one! Every effort was made to ensure it is full of as much useful information as possible, please enjoy!

CHAPTER 1

What Is Stress ?

Stress is something we all feel on a daily basis, whether we realize it or not. It is a reaction to your daily routine and unexpected bumps in the road. It is your body's response to environmental stressors, both big and small. The body needs stress responses to react to possible threats. This is a natural, primal response that began with early humans, and has kept us safe for thousands of years.

Going way back, early humans had a very short list of threats. They worried about where their next meal came from and how to stay away from predators. The stress response prompted a reaction as a necessity for survival. They did not worry about getting to soccer practice on time and paying the bills. Unfortunately for modern humans, the stress response still exists, often causing unnecessary reactions to less life-threatening situations like problems at work or fighting with a spouse. These days, think of stress as a symptom of something that is unsatisfying in your life. Whether unhappiness with your job, financial or living situation and relationships may be prompting a response to get out of the trouble you are in.

Two types of stress exist: acute, or short term, and chronic, or long term. More and more people are suffering from chronic stress, but often have acute bouts of stress on top of their usual. As stress mounts and becomes overwhelming, panic attacks and breakdown happens. Our job is to manage stress as it comes to avoid the buildup that leads to a breakdown.

Acute stress. Have you ever noticed that when you are stuck in traffic and your anxiety is high, your focus gets sharper and you think only of the task at hand? This is your stress response kicking in, giving you the mental clarity and focus needed to deal with a lifethreatening situation. It may not be actually life threatening, but your body may think so.

Episodes of acute stress tend to string together. Think about stressors
at home, work and in your social life. While these things are individually taxing, together, they add up to low level chronic

stress. Learning to handle these individual situations in a more healthy way can decrease overall chronic stress.

Chronic stress is something we all feel every day. It is the result of the alarm clock going off, getting the kids ready for school and fighting traffic to get to work on time. Small moments of stress are needed to get your body in gear and boost energy to focus on the task at hand. Most people are under a veil of chronic stress all day long.

The body responds to stress in a number of ways. First, it releases adrenaline, frequently called the body's ‚stress hormone'. It is released by the adrenal glands to raise the heart rate, blood pressure and shortens breath to take in more oxygen for the body to use. The response goes back to our primal instincts. The body needs to
prepare to run from danger, or stand and fight, the so-called ‚fight or flight' response.

Cortisol is another stress hormone that is expressed with adrenaline. While a little cortisol once in a while is a good thing, persistent exposure to cortisol, like with several small episodes of chronic stress, has some negative effects on the body. It increases blood sugar, which can lead to diabetes over time. It decreases thyroid function, cognitive function and immune system support after prolonged bouts of stress.

The most advertised impact of cortisol is its ability to store excess belly fat. When the body thinks its survival is at stake, it will take measures to store as much energy in fat as it can. Stubborn belly fat is a common symptom of chronic stress. The adrenal glands themselves can also be affected. Adrenal fatigue happens when the glands are forced to produce excessive amounts of adrenaline, cortisol and other stress hormones as a response to stress. Over time, too little hormones are made and the body suffers from extreme fatigue, slowing metabolism and suppressed immune system.

As this continues, overall mood and attitude become affected. You become more irritable, less able to focus, and it becomes increasingly more difficult to deal with minor stresses. It will become difficult to sleep, leaving you more fatigued during the day.

The less energy you have, the more susceptible you are to stress. It is a vicious circle that can only be stopped by eliminating the source of the problem, your

stress levels.

The only way to stop these negative effects is to decrease overall amounts of stress in your life. While avoiding it completely is not always possible, eliminating some sources of stress and learning to cope with unavoidable stress in a healthy way will reward you with better health overall.

Hopefully the stress of hearing about what causes stress will be the prompt you need to work on management. From here on out, we will focus on ways to deal with everyday situations in a meaningful way that reduces stress. First off, it is important to recognize possible stressors in your life. They can come from a number of places, or from one thing in particular. Common problems people face are the

following:

- Family life-difficult extended family members, children and spouses can test your patience on a daily basis. While a particular person may not be the problem, making sure everyone is happy and taken care of and where they need to be can be a stressful daily task.

- Health-declining and health are a major concern. There may not be anything you can do about your own health, or that of a loved one, and that causes anxiety for the future.
- Money-worrying about paying bills and making ends meet plagues most people. Money is the key to keeping a roof over your head and food on the table.
- Work-getting along with co-workers plus increasingly demanding jobs and deadlines often push stress levels through the roof. Not to mention the stress of commuting to and from work in heavy traffic.
- Chores and household duties. If there seems to be a never ending pile of dirty laundry and dishes, you're not alone. There will always be chores to be done, and keeping on top of them can be taxing.

CHAPTER 2
Process Stress In A Healthy Way – Eliminate Unnecessary Sources Of Stress

It is easy to turn to quick fixes to deal with stress. Crutches like smoking cigarettes and drinking alcohol seem to help calm your nerves, but only temporarily. Nicotine is an addictive drug that releases dopamine in the brain. Dopamine is a feel-good chemical that makes the stresses of life seem less severe. Smoking a cigarette is only a temporary solution, as when the dopamine wears off and the problem has not been solved, stress will begin to build up again.

Most people know that smoking is harmful to their health, yet choose to continue smoking because they are addicted, and they think it helps them deal with the problem. On the contrary, it is only good for self soothing, and when it wears off, you still have a problem to deal with.

Alcohol is very similar. It a system depressant, calming and relaxing nerves and muscles. It alters the mind so that problems don't appear as bad, and can be a temporary escape.

Unfortunately for smokers and drinkers, that temporary relaxed state is no match for the actual physical damage that they do to the body. Nicotine and alcohol are both toxic to the body. They both cause oxidative stress that begins to damage cells, and can lead to cancer over time. Alcohol also destroys the liver, the main filter keeping your blood clean.

Caffeine should be avoided during stress as well. While it is not as detrimental as smoking or drinking, caffeine is an addictive stimulant that can create hyperactivity in a person. Stress is associated with increased adrenaline, heart rate and more energy as is. Adding caffeine to the mix can increase the heart rate more, make you feel jittery and possibly lead to a panic attack. The body can only handle so much stimulation at a time, so let stress be the only factor.

Prolonged exposure to either nicotine or alcohol is detrimental to health, and could cause psychological trauma as well as physical disease. If either one of these things is your coping mechanism for stress, it is time to rethink it. Depending on how addicted you are to either substance, it may be necessary to get outside help to decrease and quit your habit. If you are a moderate user, it is possible to cut back a little at a time, and substitute healthier habits instead of alcohol or nicotine when you are stressed.

The only real way to eliminate stress is to eliminate its source. While this I not always possible, like if stress comes from a job you cannot quit, it is important to develop healthy coping mechanisms to calm you down. Start by eliminating any cause of stress that can be eliminated. Most people find they are stressed when they over extend themselves, saying yes to too many projects all at once. Know your limits, and learn to say no to people if you feel overwhelmed.

Lots of people also feel stressed by their living situations, relationships or financial circumstances. Sometimes the only way to relieve that stress is to face it head on. For example, if you have a large debt on your credit card, it is best not to ignore it. Figuring out a payment plan, even if you are paying a small amount every week, makes you feel more in control of your situation, therefore relieving stress. Sometimes not knowing the solution to your problem is more stressing than the problem itself.

There are lots of stressful situations that cannot be avoided. For example, having a sick family member is not something you cannot necessarily solve, you really just need to cope. Having healthy coping mechanisms is the key to getting through it. Here are a few examples.

Talking it out: Whether you choose to talk with a trusted friend or a professional, voicing your problems and getting it out of your head can help relieve some of the stress. It feels better knowing that someone knows what you are dealing with. It is even better if they can help come up with a solution to the problem when possible. Keeping emotions in is never a good idea, and can lead to resentment of people around you. If they do not know what your problems are, how can they help you?

Writing and journaling: If you are uncomfortable talking to others about your problems, try journaling. Getting your thoughts down on paper help you sort through them. Writing daily can help you maintain stress levels over time.

Music and Movies: using media to help you escape temporarily from your problems is a good solution. Listening to calming music or watching a funny movie can help lift your spirits and temporarily relieve stress. While it will not help solve your problem, it can keep you from overloading and having a possible panic attack. Try listening to nature sounds or classical music without words. Lyrics sometimes make things worse if a song reminds you of someone you lost or a bad time in your life. If they must have words, make sure the lyrics are happy and uplifting during times of stress.

Exercising: As we will discuss in Chapter 5, exercise can be used for stress relief. While exercise has a proven physiological benefit to reduce stress, just the act of it helps as well. Getting out for a walk, taking in some fresh air is sometimes all your mind needs to take a break and recharge. During exercise, your body takes in more oxygen, helping recharge the brain. Practicing calming techniques like yoga an Qigong help rearrange your thoughts and give more mental clarity.

Gardening, crafts and hobbies: Taking up a hobby you enjoy, especially something you can do physically, like gardening or sewing, can temporarily remove you from a stressful situation. While you can't necessarily use them to cope with acute causes of stress, like deadlines at work, doing something you enjoy when you get home will help improve your mood and outlook on your situation. Working mindlessly weeding the garden or sewing a familiar stitch allows your mind to wander, contemplating possible solutions to your problems.

Doing something productive that you like also makes you feel like you have accomplished something and if you feel stuck in a stressful situation, like waiting for someone to buy the house you are selling, can make you feel like you did something.

CHAPTER 3
Manage Stress With Food

Many people use food as a form of comfort, often overeating high fat and high sugar foods. Weight gain can certainly occur, but these types of food actually create more stress on the body. You have probably heard about allergic reactions to certain foods in the form of breaking out in hives or the throat closing up. This is the body's anaphylactic reaction to trigger foods, and there are immediate signs
that something is wrong. Some foods, however, trigger a much slower, less noticeable response that occurs in the gut. There are a few common triggers, including gluten, dairy and soy, that damage the gut lining a little at a time. Often, symptoms do not develop right away, even years after.

These triggers, and others stimulate the release of zonulin, a protein in the body that triggers gut cells to absorb nutrients. Zonulin can become over triggered if you eat the food too often. If the gut cells continue to let in goods into the bloodstream, there are likely to be pathogenic, or just unrecognizable particles entering the blood. If the immune system does not recognize something, it attacks it. When the immune system is on high alert, the body becomes unnecessarily stressed, leading to fatigue and immune burn out. So, if you are already suffering from stress at work or in your personal life, reaching for comfort foods will likely only make your problems worse.

As gluten, dairy and soy are the most common trigger, although there are others, reducing them in your diet can help your body remain healthy and deal with stress more efficiently. This means avoiding things like, ice cream, sugary cereal, processed snacks, and junk food in general. All of these products contain at least one, if not all three of the common triggers, plus artificial colorings, preservatives and excess stabilizing chemicals that cause harm and stress on the body as well. Cutting them out will help increase the efficiency of your body, giving you more energy to lead an active life and manage stress.

Reach instead for foods that are naturally anti-inflammatory like fresh fruits, vegetables and meats. The simpler the food, the less likely it is to contain inflammatory substances and chemically derived preservatives. Eat a well rounded diet to make sure you are getting the proper amount and wide variety of nutrients. It's also important to balance each meal to manage your blood sugar. If out of whack, your blood sugar can spike and drop, creating a hormonal imbalance in the body.

To maintain balance, always pair a carbohydrate-rich food, like grains and fruits, with protein, like meat or nuts, or fat, like avocado
and coconut. Carbohydrates should never be eaten alone, as they spike blood sugar quickly, then drop quickly, leaving you fatigued and hungry again. Eating protein or fat along with a carbohydrate slows the increase of blood sugar because they are digested and absorbed slower.

The type of fat also matters. Pick foods that are rich in Omega 3 fatty acids like olive oil, avocado, coconut and coconut oil and fish. These fats are anti-inflammatory, unlike Omega 6 fatty acids that are inflammatory, and found in butter, canola oil and corn oil. While Omega 6 fats cannot be avoided altogether, it is best to eat more Omega 3's than Omega 6's to decrease inflammation and stress damage to your body.

Timing of meals and snacks is also very important. Make sure to eat something every 3 to 4 hours to maintain your blood sugar. Avoid having full meals that make you feel overstuffed, and go easy on your carbohydrate portions. Small, more frequent meals keep the metabolism active and running without overloading it. If you have ever overeaten, which we all do occasionally, you may have noticed feeling fatigued and groggy afterward.

Having smaller meals more often gives your body just what it needs to keep going without weighing you down. The point of consuming food in its most basic sense is to provide what your body's cells need to create energy for your daily activities. Give your body the foods it wants to create the best energy without clogging up your system with inflammatory foods that just slow you down.

Use the following sample meal ideas to get started. Consulting with a health professional about proper meals and portions for you can also help set you up for success.

Breakfast ideas:

- Two eggs cooked with olive oil (if any), sautéed peppers, mushrooms, onions and potato hash. May use any vegetables. Substitute potato with another carb, like gluten free toast if desired.
- One serving of plain, cooked oats (no sugar added). Mix with almond milk, 2-3 tablespoons of slivered almonds plus vanilla extract and cinnamon to taste. May try flax or chia seed, almond butter in place of slivered almonds.

Morning snack ideas:

- Apple plus 1-2 tablespoons peanut butter
- 4-5 gluten and soy free crackers with 2 slices lunch meat
- ½ cup fruit of choice with 1-2 tablespoons nuts

- Lunch ideas:

- Garden salad with grilled chicken, olive oil drizzle and vinegar for dressing. May substitute tuna or lunchmeat in
- place of grilled chicken.
- Lettuce wraps with lunchmeat and cut vegetables. Use olive
- oil or avocado slices for dressing.
- Afternoon snack ideas:
- Fruit and nut bar (Larabar is gluten, dairy and soy free)
- 4-5 gluten and soy free crackers with 1-2 tablespoons peanut or almond butter.
- ¼ cup hummus plus carrot sticks

Dinner ideas:

- Baked or grilled salmon with asparagus and baked potato. Use olive or coconut oil to sautee asparagus.
- Pasta night- Marinara sauce with ground beef or turkey over small helping of gluten free pasta. Use spaghetti squash or zucchini noodles as a substitute for paste. Serve with a side
- salad.
- Steak with broccoli and rice.

Dessert ideas:

- Fruit with natural cocoa spread (should be soy and dairy free)
- Dark chocolate square with small serving of fruit
- Dried cranberry or raisin with nuts

Getting your diet under control will help maintain or lose weight, stabilize your blood sugar and lower inflammation in your body. It is important to feed your body properly so that it may function at optimal levels. It will repay you by giving more energy, more mental clarity and function, and will be less affected by outside stress.

CHAPTER 4
Manage Stress with Exercise

The benefits to exercise are seemingly endless. Being active lowers blood pressure, cholesterol, blood sugar levels as well as keeping muscles strong, including your heart.

When it comes to stress, exercise helps for a number of reasons. First is the anecdotal benefit of getting your problems off your mind, or at least giving you the chance to think them through. Going for a long, leisurely walk gives your mind time to wander, and often gives the walker a little bit of clarity in dealing with whatever stressful situation they happen to be dealing with. This works especially well for people that are constantly moving from one thing to another, like in fast-paced work environments. The mind has no distractions
except the sound of footsteps, forcing it to slow, process and rest.

More involved exercise, like an aerobics class or yoga seems to give the brain rest as well. All mental focus has to be trained on the task

at hand to do all the moves in aerobics or yoga. The mind concentrates on body position and coordination, rather than deadlines and bottom
lines.

Exercise is important on a cellular level as well. During exercise, the hormone norepinephrine is released, which moderates body's stress response. It is a stress hormone, just like adrenaline and cortisol, yet its function is really to create awareness and mental clarity in the mind, so that it may react quickly and appropriately to a stressful
situation.

Exercise also releases endorphins, or happy hormones that increase feelings of satisfaction and happiness, the exact opposite feelings stress is associated with. They help reduce the body's perception of pain and often act like a sedative. While these effects can also be seen from a cocktail of prescription medication, exercise is the natural way to boost your feel-good hormones.

Stressful situations naturally cause the release of adrenaline, the hormone that preps body muscles to run away from a threat. This is a primal response that doesn't always work well in modern times. Most likely, you will not be running away from your desk and your boss or your family commitments. Or should you? That adrenaline will sit idle in your muscles until it is used, making you feel tense and edgy. A bit of exercise uses up that adrenaline, making you feel more calm.

Just about any exercise will do, as long as it is done consistently throughout the week and you don't over do it. As with any new exercise routine, it is important to know your limits and build your stamina over time, rather than doing too much and adding more unnecessary stress on your body. Here are a few types of exercise to try adding to your daily routine.

Cardio-walking, jogging or running will give you the immediate adrenaline release you need to calm down and refocus your attention on the task at hand. Making sure to do this daily, or every other day helps maintain stress levels. Using it as a coping mechanism during particularly stressful times is also much better than turning to food, cigarettes or alcohol.

If you are not used to running or walking, take it slow. Any bit of exercise will make improvements in your stress level, so even a quick 5-minute walk around your office building with help reduce your worries. As you build stamina, increase the time or the intensity of exercise for added benefits.

Yoga- known for its mind/body benefits, yoga is a great, low impact exercise to start incorporating. There are several forms of yoga, but all are centered around specific body poses that are held to stretch and increase muscle strength to relieve stress. Poses vary from standing, sitting and laying down. You will be taught to breathe a little differently while holding poses, allowing for a better stretch and strengthening of muscles. The practice of deep breathing in itself is calming, which will be discussed more in Chapter 10. It is meant to be calming and relaxing, and is not a test of flexibility. The idea of 'practicing' yoga is to improve upon your own strength and

flexibility, not to compete with others.

If you are not familiar with yoga, taking an introductory class is the best place to start. Online tutorials are okay, but it takes too much focus to pay attention to your computer screen. Taking a class allows you to simply listen to instructions and take an occasional glance at your instructor to make sure you're doing it right.

Try a beginners class first. Advanced classes and hot yoga classes are meant for those who already have a good idea of what to do. While not hard, it adds another level of focus and capability you may not have as a beginner. Taking an introductory class gives you time to learn some standard poses and get into the swing of things. You will
likely feel much less stress after your first class, but if you don't, try it again.

The stress of trying something new could hinder your first try. Also, make sure you find a teacher that you are comfortable with, as technique can vary, and you may find that some teachers explain less and move quicker through poses.

After you learn some things, you will likely have a few poses that you like best, and these could always become your go-to poses to do at home, or when you are feeling particularly stressed.

Tai Chi- this ancient Chinese practice is like yoga, but with more fluid movement. It is sometimes referred to as 'meditation in motion'. While its exact origins are unknown, it is said it was developed to be a branch of martial arts. Regular practice promotes overall wellness through better flexibility, balance, increased feelings of inner peace and less depression. Since it involves fluid motion, it does add a level of cardio workout, although light, and is low impact
for joints.

Medical studies link practice of Tai Chi to decreased symptoms of Parkinsons, diabetes and fibromyalgia, and decreases the risk of chronic heart failure and depression.

Motions are meant to be done fluidly, meaningfully and without break. There are several offshoot techniques, each a little different, but rooted in the same concept. Just like yoga, a beginners class to learn the basics is a great place to start.

Qigong- another Chinese-derived exercise is a combination of yoga and Tai Chi. It combines the breathing exercises of yoga with the fluid motion of Tai Chi. There are several types, including a hardcore martial arts version, but the most commonly known practice is for stress relief, joint pain reduction and balance. Like Tai Chi, consistent practice shows considerable improvement in conditions like arthritis, pain, cancer and overall stress. Followers attest to having more energy and more tolerance to stress.

Whatever type of exercise you choose, make sure to start small and not over tax your body. Pick something that fits relatively well with your daily routine so that the stress of adding another thing to your to do list doesn't bring you down. The exercise must be enjoyable. We are trying to increase levels of happiness, not bring you down.

CHAPTER 5

Manage Stress With Sleep

Sleep, as a definition, is a mental state where your body is relaxed and still, and your mind, body and soul are given time to recharge. You should be getting 7-10 hours of restful sleep per night to be fully charged in the morning. There are several factors that can cut this time short, stress being a major factor.

As you sleep, your brain goes through several cycles of REM sleep, deep sleep cycles that recharge the brain with oxygen, allowing cells to recover. Interestingly enough, a REM cycle is associated with vivid
dreams, eye movement under the lids, which would seem like a restless sleep. The REM cycle occurs toward waking hours which is why it is important to get uninterrupted sleep to facilitate this process.

If you are stressed, you are probably either get too little sleep, have a hard time falling asleep and wake up groggy and tired. Like we said before, chronic stress causes the release of adrenaline, and unless you do something about it, will make you feel edgy and tense. This only goes away by using the adrenaline that has already been produced, and stopping the addition of more by getting your stressors under control. Easier said than done, but lots of little changes to your bedtime routine can help you sleep better.

Reducing stressors before bed: The only real way to cut off stress is to stop thinking about the thing that is bothering you. Avoid going to bed feeling tense and awake. Your muscles should be relaxed and your mind turned off. That may seem unreasonable, as you have undoubtedly tried, but try these few things to alleviate your stress.

- Cut off all electronic use at least an hour before bedtime, no cell phones or computers specifically. The glow of artificial light from phones and TVs keeps you up, and if you choose to look at work items, will keep you up longer. Unplug.
- Read a leisure book or magazine. Pick up a paper copy of something you have wanted to read. Pick a book that is unrelated to your daily tasks, like a fiction novel, that can take your mind to a completely different place.

- Practice yoga poses before bed. Take a few minutes to do some of your favorite poses to focus your breathing and release some stress from your muscles.
- Write to relax. Sometimes getting your thoughts down on paper helps clarify your thoughts. Whether it is writing through an emotional situation or simply making a list of things you don't want to forget tomorrow at work, doing something physical and tangible seems to give the brain some relief.
- Try deep breathing to calm yourself. The practice of deep breathing helps focus the mind on just breathing, rather than other things. As your mind eases, you will be able to drift off.

Specific exercises will be discussed in Chapter 10.

While these techniques might not work for everyone, or in every situation, they are a good start. Consider the possibility that you have a functional issue with rest. You may have trouble sleeping because you had caffeine too late in the day, or because your body's natural circadian rhythm is disrupted. Your body is designed to release melatonin and taurine at specific times to put you to sleep.

Should that rhythm be off, it will be difficult to sleep until this balance is corrected. Melatonin and taurine supplements are available to try. In general, melatonin helps you fall asleep and taurine helps you stay asleep. Try one based on which problem you are having. Always check with your doctor to determine if supplementation is safe for you.

Medications are also available over the counter and by prescription to help you sleep immediately however, they have many negative side effects including waking groggy and sleep walking. Doesn't sound like you will be getting much beneficial rest with these, and they can be habit forming. It's best to stick to natural solutions whenever possible.

Another possibility is that you have sleep apnea. Most sufferers do not realize they have it, but it greatly effects quality of sleep. Sleep apnea is a condition where breathing is halted and oxygen is decreased to the brain. The decrease in oxygen causes the person to feel groggy and tired upon waking, as their brain has not fully recharged.

The affected sometimes appear to stop breathing, then suddenly take a gasping deep breath, all while asleep. This problem is common, but not limited to, people who are overweight or obese. Excess weight can cause pressure on the lungs and trachea, making it harder to breathe. Structural abnormalities could also cause it.

Snoring is another common symptom. This condition is dangerous, and should be treated properly. If a family member has complained that you snore, don't just brush it off. It could be a symptom of sleep apnea. Mention it to you doctor so that they may do appropriate testing to diagnose. Use of a CPAP machine pumps extra oxygen into the lungs through a breathing mask worn at night.

Your sleeping environment plays a big role in restful sleep as well. A deep, restful sleep without interruptions can be difficult to get. Light and noise pollution as well as restless pets and children can keep you

from getting a full 8 hours of sleep. While these things are unavoidable, they do lead to increased stress during the day.

You can at least work on the things you can control. For example, the temperature in the room is important because you could either be too cold or too hot, prompting addition and subtraction of blankets all night long. Most people prefer a cooler room, so that they may have a blanket on and not be too hot.

Light and sound can be controlled to a point as well. Addition of white noise, either from a specifically programmed sound machine, or something as simple as a ceiling or stand alone fan can create a hum that blocks out all other external sounds. Use heavy shades or sleeping masks to block out all light. The idea is to turn off the senses of sight and sound that keep the brain active longer than necessary. Using aromatherapy scents like lavender also have a calming effect on the mind, which may lull you to sleep faster. More on that in
Chapter 12.

CHAPTER 6
Manage Stress With Meditation

Meditation is a powerful tool for stress relief and management. Meditation, in its simplest terms, is practicing to become more mindful. While there are several offshoots, which will be discussed, the general idea is to sit still and maintain your focus on one single thought. Whether that be a sound, your breath, or a mantra, the idea is to focus your attention and stop thinking about the stressors in your life.

Meditation originated in Hindu culture over 5,000 years ago, although most researchers believe it started long before this, but written word does not go back that far. Carved figures were found by archaeologists working in the Indus Valley in the early 1900's showing meditation poses and Sanskrit words for chanting. Hinduism was the first major religion to practice meditation. Buddhism was later developed, centered around the meditation practice for spiritual enlightenment.

Similar practices developed in other regions around the world, including North America. Native Americans used meditation techniques involving high heat to create a heightened sense of awareness in sweat lodges. They would also dance to drums, entering a trance-like state. A similar practice in Istanbul, the Sufi Whirling Dervish dance, where people listen to music, internally recite prayer and spin in circles is meant to let go of inhibitions and connect a person to their inner self. The rituals and movements also have several other religious aspects, a testament to the God, Allah.

The Aborigines in Australia used sound techniques from didgeridoos, and Islamic and Christian prayer was, and still is a form of meditation. The need for spiritual enlightenment and centering is something all humans share. While we may each do it in a different way, we are all connected by the search for spiritual enlightenment.

Two main types of practice exist, upward meditation and downward meditation. The idea of upward meditation is that energy is drawn up and out of the body through meditation creating a so-called out of body experience. The mind becomes detached from the body. Downward meditation does the opposite, bringing energy into the body, giving a higher sense of connection between the mind and body.

There are many ways to use meditation for specific purposes. For the beginner, the purpose is usually to relieve stress and focus on positivity. More specific practices get the meditator to get in touch with their emotions, or focus on the realities of life, or the opposite, provide an escape with fantastic methods. Meditation can be used as therapy for a number of conditions, prompting the meditator to get in touch with thoughts and emotions, and work through them in their own mind. This is part of the process to enlightenment.

Meditation has so many benefits in stress management and in other aspects of life. People who practice report having a greater sense of inner peace. This often stems from lower blood pressure, decreased tensing of muscles, decreased restlessness and better sleep. All of these things reduce the total stress on the body, allowing it to function properly and handle stress as it comes in a more effective way. A study done by Harvard in the 1970s created and tested methods of meditation and found tangible ways to measure these successes of meditation. Their participants were less anxious, able to accomplish more during the day and had lower risk for medical ailments like heart disease and depression.

A word of caution when exploring your meditation options. Meditation is an individual process. It only requires your mind, body and focus. Be weary of practitioners who tell you that other things, like special mats or candles or tapes and videos are required. They may just be looking to sell you something that will not necessarily enhance your meditation process.

Other practitioners may want to try and convert you to a new religion or spiritual practice. While exploring these options is a necessary step to enlightenment, if you feel uncomfortable in any way, or feel that a practitioner is motivated by anything other than your well being, you have the right to cease the relationship. Research and read reviews if you decide paying for a class is the right option for you. Find out before investing if the service you are signing up for is worth the money.

Heart Rhythm Meditation: this method is downward centered, creating more awareness and energy inside the body. Listening to your heartbeat, rather than your breath is better for some people, because sometimes your breath becomes controlled, and quickens the more you focus on it. People report quickening breath leading to panic attacks when they focus on it too much. The heartbeat is less changed by focusing on it, making it a better pulse point for attention.

Simply sit in an upright position, close your eyes and place the fingers from one hand on the wrist of the other. Press gently and feel your pulse, and let this sensation be your guide to focus your attention. As you feel the heartbeat, internally hear the words ‚Sat Nam' for the contraction and relaxation of your heart.

Mantra meditation: The idea of mantra meditation is to focus your thoughts on one singular word or sound. The sound is externalized and chanted. You commonly hear the chant ‚Aum' or ‚Ohm'. The chant is meant to be a primal sound that, when chanted, resonates through the entire body. It can be felt as a vibration in the body that creates a sense of calm, relaxation, and focus only on this sound. As you say it, do not try to reach a certain octave or note, simply let it flow from your lungs. The note should feel natural and deep coming from your throat. There really is no right way to do this, as long as it feels calming and relaxing to you. This practice can be done as part of a guided class, but the chanting of others around you can become distracting. However, others feel that chanting as a community offers different sensations that can be beneficial as well.

Transcendental Meditation: This is an offshoot of mantra meditation, in which a specific process was created by one practitioner. Maharishi Mahesh Yogi. To quote him,

,THE GOAL OF TRANSCENDENTAL MEDITATION IS THE STATE OF ENLIGHTENMENT. THIS MEANS WE EXPERIENCE THAT INNER CALMNESS, THAT QUIET STATE OF LEAST EXCITATION, EVEN WHEN WE ARE DYNAMICALLY BUSY'. STRESS MUST BE RELIEVED IN ORDER TO ACHIEVE SPIRITUAL ENLIGHTENMENT, AND THAT IS DONE THROUGH
MEDITATION.

As the most recognizable type of meditation, this involves sitting still in the lotus position and chanting an internal mantra. Usually, you will focus on one specific word that has a neutral meaning, something that doesn't evoke any particular emotion. The word itself does not matter.

The word should be said internally, repeated at a pace that keeps your focused on the word, with no mind wandering. For example, should you say ‚faithful' as your word, give it a few seconds before you say it again. Keep this pace for a minute, and if your mind begins to wander at this pace, say it with less space between. This will help keep your focus on the single word, rather than slipping back into thoughts of the day.

There are many classes available that teach the process of Transcendental Meditation, but the description above is pretty much it. This can be done anywhere, like in a quiet room at home, or in your office chair at work. The environment and the position in which you do this are less important than maintaining the overall focus. Classes may be helpful for some if they do not have an environment to meditate in that is quiet and free from external distractions. Sometimes getting out of the physical area where stress occurs helps the process significantly.

Several sources say that practicing this technique for about 15 minutes 2-3 times per day for the best results. When practiced regularly, followers experience less stress overall, more mental clarity and a greater awareness of the world around them.

Passive meditation: This method is probably one of the easiest to begin with. A sound, like a gong or bell can be used to create a steady repeating sound. The meditator simply has to focus on this external sound, rejecting all other thoughts. The only downfall for this type of guided meditation is that it may not work for each individual in every situation. Unlike transcendental meditation, the meditator relies on an outside source for their focus sound, rather than creating it from within. It does not allow for change in the sound, or change in frequency. Depending on your mental state, your mind may wander if it cannot fully engage in the sound provided.

The nice thing is, you can use pre-recorded sounds at home to create a more calming environment. Should the sound not work for you on a particular day, change or add your own internal mantra to help focus your mind.

Mindfulness: this technique is different from the rest, and rejects the idea that you must focus on one thing to escape from stress in your life. In this method, sitting still and letting any and all thoughts enter your head allows you to time to think, but not act. This method is incredible useful in work environments. You can sit for 5 or 10 minutes simply thinking about the task at hand before saying or doing anything. Sometimes this is the mental clarity you need to continue on with confidence.

You are invited to try all types of meditation in order to find what works best for you. Many people try one type, decide it is not for them, and simply give up. Try several things, like you would with exercise classes before you make that decision. Finding a method, whether it be one of these or a combination of methods is highly individual, and can also develop and change for each person over time. There are no rights and wrongs to meditation. Trying to fit a particular mold may actually create more stress, so just do what is comfortable for you.

CHAPTER 7

Guided 5-Minute Meditation Session

Try this 5-minute guided meditation to calm yourself during stressful situation. This short practice will help you gather your thoughts and calm your breathing. This can be done as a guided meditation, by listening to this audio book, or these techniques can easily be translated into a self-guided process to use at your desk at work, in the car or at home. Let's begin.

Start by getting in a comfortable position. Sit so your back, hips and legs are comfortable and not strained. You may sit cross-legged, legs straight or in a chair. Center your spine over your hips, straight up, head straight and in line with your spine. Imagine a string is holding your head and spine, pulling it upward toward the sky. Close your eyes.

Take a deep breath in, hold it for a moment, then release slowly, feeling the pressure and anxiety being released with your breath. Continue breathing normally, in and out.

Feel your breath slow as you begin to relax.

Focus on your finger tips. Feel the energy pulse through them as you remain still.

Focus on your toes. Feel the energy pulse through them as you remain still. Slowly move your hands to your stomach. Gently place your palms on your belly.

Feel your belly expand as you steadily breathe in and out. Feel the energy flowing between your palms and belly.

Sit like this in silence for a few moments. Let any thought that enters your mind to linger there. Do not force them out or try to change them, just listen to your inner thoughts.

When you're ready, slowly open your eyes.

Remain still for a moment as you re-enter your world.

Begin again refreshed and awake.

Repeat this mini-session any time you are feeling fatigued or overwhelmed. Pair it with longer meditation sessions for a better sense of inner peace every day.

CHAPTER 8

Guided 20 Minute Meditations Ession

Try this guided meditation session daily, multiple times daily if needed. Practice first thing in the morning before you start your day to get a renewed sense of focus and purpose for the day. This may also be done at night to calm your nerves and prepare you for sleep. Find a quiet space in your home free of external distractions like light and sound. The room should be dimly lit, allowing for your eyes to relax. It should also be free of irregular sounds. If necessary, try running a fan or other white noise to create a steady sound that is less jarring. The room should be a comfortable temperature, you should not be hot or cold. It is only distracting. Ask others around you to give you the quiet time you need, so that your session is not interrupted. Let us begin.

Start by getting in a comfortable position. Sit so your back, hips and legs are comfortable and not strained. You may sit cross-legged, legs straight or in a chair. Center your spine over your hips, straight up, head straight and in line with your spine. Imagine a string is holding your head and spine, pulling it upward toward the sky. Close your eyes.

Take a deep breath in, hold it for a moment, then release slowly, feeling the pressure and anxiety being released with your breath. Sit still for a moment, taking note of the slowing of your breath as you relax. Now I want you to focus your attention on a single word. "peaceful". This word will symbolize your state of mind, the state of your body and your only intention from this moment forward. It is everything. Say the word to yourself in your mind.

What feelings does this word bring forward?
Peaceful (wait 3 seconds), peaceful (wait 3 seconds), peaceful (wait 3 seconds, repeat for 2-3 minutes. Stay silent for another minute) Slowly take a deep breath in, hold it for a moment, then release slowly, feeling the pressure and anxiety being released with your breath.

Take a moment to feel the energy pulsing through your body. Focus on the top of your head. Feel the energy move down your spine. Feel the pulsing energy as it rushes toward your fingertips. Feel it course through your legs, extending all the way down to your toes. Feel it come back up as it circles through your heart, your organs, bringing fresh life.

Slowly take a deep breath in, hold it for a moment, then release slowly, feeling the pressure and anxiety being released with your breath.

Let your mind relax, focusing only on the sound of my voice. Know that at this moment, you are perfectly calm. You are solely in control of your body, your mind and your surroundings. Nothing can touch the power inside of you. You can move the Earth. You create the breeze that is blowing through the trees. You are the energy that moves rivers of water. The tide that makes waves slowly breaking on the beach. You are the creator of all energy. Everything is under your control.

Slowly take a deep breath in, hold it for a moment, then release slowly, feeling the pressure and anxiety being released with your breath.

Sit in silence and allow in any thought that comes to mind. Do not try to suppress any thought, let it linger, grow and change.

(moment of silence for 4-5 minutes) Slowly take a deep breath in, hold it for a moment, then release slowly, feeling the pressure and anxiety being released with your breath.

In a few moments we will say, "Aum". Take a deep breath and create sound as you exhale. Let the sound flow through you, taking its natural course. Let it sound how it wants to sound.

Now take a deep breath and say "Aum". Let the sound continue until you run out of breath.

Again, breathe in and exhale "Aum".

Slowly take a deep breath in, hold it for a moment, then release slowly, feeling the pressure and anxiety being released with your breath.

Slowly open your eyes but focus only on the sound of my voice. You will now begin again. You are relaxed, calm and confident. Wherever you go from here, you are in control. You are in charge of your own destiny.

Your problems are but small pebbles on a sandy beach. They can simply be washed away with the waves you have created.

Go forth renewed, relaxed and clear.

CHAPTER 9

Manage Stress With Deep Breathing Exercises

Deep breathing is really the center of all relaxation practices. From yoga to meditation and aroma therapy, focus on the inhale and exhale of breath is used to control anxiety levels and create a sense of calm in the body.

The nice thing about deep breathing exercises is the ability to do it just about anywhere. Certain methods require you to be in certain positions, but they can be modified to be done spur of the moment at your office or in the car if necessary.

Simply focus on your breath, in and out. Sit with your back in good posture, or lay flat on your back. Place one hand on your chest and one on your stomach. Take a few breaths normally and pay attention where your breath comes from, either the belly or the chest. It comes from the chest in most people. As you become conscious of this, focus on taking deep breaths that fill your belly. Use your abdominal muscles to pull as much air in as possible, then release slowly, allowing your muscles to push out every last bit of air.

As more oxygen enters your system, your brain will recharge, your heart rate will slow, and you will become more relaxed. Repeat each session for about five minutes any time you are feeling stressed for a breath of fresh air. This can be done in the office, at home or in the car (while it's in park!).

CHAPTER 10

Maintain Activities With Positive People

Many people tend to shy away from their usual activities when they are stressed, anxious or depressed. They feel they cannot handle any more stimulation, and often choose to be solitary. The tendency to withdraw from social situations is actually detrimental to the situation, especially with depression. Sometimes it can be difficult to pick yourself up and force yourself to get out to a party, or even have lunch with a friend, but the healthy benefits it provides once you get there are usually immediate.

Besides stress relief, socializing has been shown to boost the immune system, fighting off the cold and flu, and may actually help you live longer. Socializing, especially in older adults keeps the brain engaged and decreases your risk of developing dementia. When it comes to stress, engaging in social activities boosts the mood and helps distract you from your problems, if only for a short time. Take time to reconnect with people, get your mind of things that are stressing you. It is so easy to get caught up in your own thoughts. The more you dwell on your negative thoughts, the bigger they become.

There is one caviot, however. The people you associate with should be positive thinking, supportive people. Hanging around with people who only want to complain about their problems, complain about other people, and have nothing to offer but negativity will not reduce your stress levels. Sometimes that means going outside your normal circle of friends to find some relief. Here are a few ideas to get out there:

Take an exercise class: Bonding with a new friend in your exercise class is a great way to break the ice. You are both there to do a positive thing, improve your health. Make it a point to say 'Hello' and introduce yourself to someone in the class. They may be looking for a new friend as well. Even if you don't talk to someone new, taking a class can still give you a sense of community you would not get from doing an exercise video alone at home, or taking a walk by yourself. Everyone in the class is there to do the same thing, and are there voluntarily. By default, you all have something in common, and that can help build new friendships.

If your social skills are more advanced, consider joining a sports team if you have the time. Playing team sports like volleyball or softball keep you engaged and constantly interacting with your teammates. You will celebrate wins together, practice together and build new relationships.

Volunteer: Whether it be at your local soup kitchen or helping organize an event, volunteering will make you feel good because you are helping other people. You will likely also be sharing your time with like-minded positive people who want to help as well.

Getting active in your community will put you face to face with someone you have yet to meet. Building friendships in the community will give you a place to turn when you are having a difficult time. You may also learn some new skills, boosting your self-confidence and mood. Everything about it says stress relief.

If you're not sure where to get started, keep an eye out on community bulletin boards and the local newspaper for advertisements of upcoming events and volunteer requests. It may be helping organize the town parade, rebuilding something, or gathering donations for a family in need. Find a cause that speaks to you so the take does not feel like work. Remember that the key to stress relief is doing something enjoyable to boost endorphins, it should not stress you out even more.

We said before that over extending yourself is often a cause of stress. Make sure the volunteer activity you decide to do fits in your schedule, and does not take more commitment than you can offer. A one-time volunteer opportunity is a good place to start. Something like raking leaves on the town green will likely take only a few hours with no other commitment. This will give you a chance to get out and do something without a long term commitment.

Networking events: Most people think of networking events as a way to get in touch with colleagues or make new customers for their business. This may not seem like a good way to relieve stress if your main issue is work. While most events like this are set up with workrelated themes, it I possible to network with people in other ways. First off, socializing with your co-workers or people in the same field as you has its benefits. If you do attend one of these events, talk only a little about your business, but spend a good deal of time trying to get to know people on a personal level. Most likely, those you speak with don't want to focus on work after hours either. Also, taking the time to know someone could inadvertently get you some new clients, as you become an approachable, relatable human being.

If your main source of stress is social anxiety, networking and carrying on a conversation with a stranger may make your blood pressure rise. While the point is to relieve stress, remember that sometimes facing your problem head on is the only way to fix it and decrease stress. For lots of people, conversation is not a natural thing. It takes mental preparation and great focus to carry it out. Think of networking as a job skill (because it really is). You did not learn how to use the computer system at work overnight, but you eventually did. The more you practice communicating with people, the better you will become, and the less stressful it will be.

If work events don't seem appetizing, think about your favorite hobby. For instance, let's say you really like knitting or crafts. Seek out a craft fair or local knitting group. Meeting people with similar interests is a great way to get the conversation started, boosting those endorphins. Picking up some new skills from new people will help increase your self confidence as well. You may even make some new friends.

Play with your pet: If interacting with humans has no appeal to you, especially if part of your stress is social anxiety, starting with a pet may be a good transition. Interacting with a dog or cat is much less taxing than carrying on a conversation with a person. Pets just like to play, get pet and snuggle. While they sometimes act up, they don't talk back, and they relieve stress.

If you have a pet already, spend some more time with them. Take your dog out for a long walk, play ball in the yard, or simply take more time to acknowledge and appreciate that they are there. Remember that your dog is always excited to see you when you get home, regardless of whether you blew a big meeting at work or not. They don't care about anything except you. Think of this often at work to lift your spirits. Think about how they jump around, wag their tails and lick you to say hello as you walk in the door. It will give you something to look forward to. Cats are great too, but their love is a bit less enthusiastic. They may just brush up against your leg or curl up next to you on the couch, but the love is the same. Many studies have shown that pet owners have less anxiety, lower blood pressure and decreased risk of depression.

Taking your dog to the dog park or out on a walk also attracts other dog loving people. Just as it is important for your dog to socialize with other dogs, you should be socializing with their owners. Simple conversations lead to play dates, a few laughs and a new friend.

If you don't have a pet, you may think about getting one, but remember that having an animal takes a commitment of time and resources. You should not get a pet if you don't have proper time to spend with it, the animal will suffer. Instead, volunteer at a local animal shelter. There, you can play with and walk dogs, or sit and snuggle with cats and kittens. While you are not committing to them long term, you can make their day, and yours by spending a little time with them.

CHAPTER 11

Daily Affirmations

Your day should revolve around positivity, and the source of that positivity must begin with you. What was the last thing you thought about yourself? Did you praise yourself for a job well done, or did you internally scold yourself for not doing something right? Would you speak to your loved one the same way if they had done something wrong? Likely not, so why would you speak to yourself that way.

It is so easy to get down on yourself for something you screwed up, or just about how you feel about yourself in general. One small negative thought can snowball in your head to become a blizzard of negativity, nit-picking every little thing about yourself. Your thought could start out as, ‚I really don't like how my body looks in this shirt.' In essence, it is really the shirt that is the problem, not your body, but what it turns in to is, ‚I don't look good in anything, I hate my body, how could anybody love me?'

While this may seem a little wild, the mind's natural process is to dwell on the little things until they become big things. It is important to remind yourself of this before your thoughts get out of control.

The mind is a very interesting thing. Your brain's nerve and thought system creates habits. It creates pathways of neurons that become familiar in order to save time and streamline the processing of thought. If your thoughts are always negative, that nerve pathway will become a highway that all your thoughts want to drive on.

It becomes your job to make your thoughts take the back roads, changing them to positive thoughts, and building up those pathways. This starts with recognizing your thoughts when they happen, and making them positive. Think of it this way. If you were to externalize your thoughts about how your body looks to your best friend, how would they respond? If you said that you were a complete failure because you messed up a project at work, they would not say, ‚Yeah, you should probably just quit because you did a terrible job'. They would say, ‚Okay, you may have screwed up that project but remember how successful you were on the last project, and the one before that? Let's find a way to fix it and make it better.' You are your own best friend. You are with yourself all the time. Give yourself the same compassion your best friend would.

Retrain your thinking by being more vigilant of your thoughts. Your subconscious thinking happens constantly, so it is your job to become more aware of the thoughts swirling around your head. To start, try to take a minute once every hour to address your internal thoughts. Have the majority of thought been positive or negative? Were the thoughts you were having rational? Often times the brain lets thoughts blow way out of proportion, and are often irrational. Get your subconscious in check by letting your rational brain decide whether those thoughts are worthy of your time.

For example, your thought may be, 'My boss is going to fire me because I failed the assignment. I won't be able to pay my mortgage, and I will get evicted. I'll have to live with my mother, and the kids will have to change school systems, and they will hate me.' Let your rational brain kick in here and bring you back to zero.

You have not been fired, therefore you still can pay the bills. None of your worst fears are happening at this time, so calm down. Go back to the original problem, the failed assignment. Figure out a way to solve your problem head on. Talk to your boss. Find a way to revamp the project to turn it into a success. Avoiding the problem and waiting to get fired is not a good solution.

Say something good to yourself when you make small accomplishments. Give yourself an internal pat on the back when you have finished the dishes, folded and put away laundry, got through a difficult meeting, made it home on time. Remember that even the small, mundane things are worthy of celebration, because for some, just getting out of bed is a major success. Remember that you have it good, and anything you do during the day is cause for a pat on the back.

Begin saying daily affirmations to yourself every morning before your day starts. What you hear within the first hour of waking up sets the tone for the whole day, so make sure it is positive. Upon waking, sit up in bed, turn on the light and look around. You woke up today on the right side of the ground, so you have to be thankful.

Also be thankful that you have a roof above your head and a bed to sleep in. You are ahead of the curve. As you begin your morning routine, take gratitude in all of the things you have. Recognize the breakfast you are eating as a gift, and as a measure of your past successes. Remember that the laundry, the sweeping and the dishes are proof that you have clothing, a house to live in and food to eat.

As you get dressed and ready, recognize that your body has carried you so far in life, and that it is a gift. It should not be criticized for being too big or having imperfections. Look at yourself in the mirror and set the tone for the day. Say, out loud, your daily affirmations:

I am strong, I am here, and I am successful. I have accomplished so much in my life, and today will be no different. I will start today with positivity. I will go through the day with energy and purpose. I will end the day feeling accomplished, but not tired. I am good enough, and nobody can take my confidence from me. I am me, and there is no equal.

Your daily affirmation can be whatever you want it to be, but it should be motivating, it should be enlightening, and it should be true. It should not be about how great your hair looks, or how nice your clothes are. It should be about your strengths as a person, not physical appearance. That can change at any time, and putting all your stock in looks and things will cause you to fail later on.

CHAPTER 12

Positive Imagery

Fill your life with positive images to back up your positive thoughts. Whether you realize it or not, everything that you experience and look at through the day has an effect on you. If you surround yourself with unpaid bills and a cluttered home, your mood will be anxious and chaotic. If you fill your surroundings with family pictures and a clean home, you will feel much more uplifted and calm. While you may not be able to fill your entire world with positive pictures, you can work on your environment, and use internal pictures for when things are out of your control.

Start with your home. Everyone should have a nice place to come home to. Paint your walls a bright, calming color. Decorate with pictures of great days with the family, and objects that make you smile or remind you of a great experience. Vacation photos and souvenirs from family outings invoke feelings that bring the experience back. Surround yourself with things with meaning. A cluttered home usually means you have a cluttered mind. Avoid having too many knick-knacks and clutter all over your home that distract your mind. Have only what you need to feel comfortable. Make an effort to get the dishes done and the laundry folded so you don't come home to a mess.

Make your office an extension of your home, if you can. Bring in pictures that remind you of nice things, and put a stamp of your personality on your space. If you don't work somewhere that you have a specific office or personal space, make the best of a locker or drawer that may be yours. Even putting a picture of your loved ones on your phone or computer to look at occasionally is a step in the right direction.

If you find yourself in a situation where there is no beauty, no positivity and no hope, turn to your mind. Your brain has the capacity to take you back to a time and place where you felt calm and serene, giving you a moment to escape and detach from your situation. This practice can be immediately calming, and will help you get through a stressful event. Take a deep breath and close your eyes.

Imagine you are home, sitting on the couch with a good book. Think about how warm you feel under a blanket, and clutching a cup of your favorite tea. Go back to that thought and remember how calm you were, with no need to get up and rush out the door. You were simply content right there, enjoying the moment.

You could also use something more generic, like thinking about something you would like to do. For example, if you have booked a vacation for later this year, use it as a tool to motivate you and get you there. Imagine you are sitting in the sand, with the warm sun on your face, listening to the waves, and the seagulls. Whatever image you use, take a few opportune moments to really develop the thought. A fleeting, waves crashing on the beach image will not do much. Take the time to think about how the sand would feel between your toes to really put yourself in a more calm frame of mind.

CHAPTER 13

Aromatherapy

Have you ever smelled something that immediately brought back a great childhood memory? Maybe the smell of fried dough at the fair, or salt air from a family vacation at the beach? The power of smell has a strong connection to memory and feeling. Negative smells from certain foods or from garbage illicit a negative emotional response as well. As far as stress relief is concerned, aromatherapy uses certain smells to give specific responses in the brain, and remind you of good memories. Certain smells also produce a calming effect on the brain as well.

The presence of any smell with cause the brain to focus on it, minimizing other thoughts. Think about how the smell of food in a restaurant can distract you from a conversation, or if the kitchen garbage smells strong enough, you must give if your full attention and take it out before you do anything else. For stress relief, the introduction of good smells like lavender or mint give the brain something positive to focus on, while giving less attention to the stressors in your life. While this may only be a temporary solution, your body will have time to regulate your blood pressure and calm your tense muscles.

Aromatherapy is commonly used in tandem with massage therapy to increase the calming effect. The smell of essential oils calms the brain while the masseuse works to relieve tension in the muscles. Scent from essential oils is also great to use at home. An oil diffuser uses heat from flame to send oil particles into the air, filling the space with the aroma. Certain scents, like lavender or chamomile are great for stress relief, but any smell that you enjoy can be used to help calm you. Oils from mint or citrus can be very uplifting and energizing to your body and spirit.

While diffusers are great, essential oils can be used in other ways as well. Potpurri made of lavender can be placed in a bedroom to help you fall asleep, and air fresheners can be used in the car to calm you while driving. Essential oils like orange and lemon are often used in cleaning products to make the home feel fresh, although they are usually filled with chemicals as well. Homemade cleaners using essential oils, vinegar and natural castile soap are a great natural alternative that you won't feel guilty about inhaling.

Add a few drops to your hot bath water to disperse scent in the air. Essential oils can also be used in place of dryer sheets that often have a very strong smell. Add a few drops on a damp washcloth and throw it in with a load of clothes. The scent will dry into the clothes, giving you fresh, calming scents all day long.

Use smell wherever you go for a relaxing boost of energy. You could even keep a bottle of your favorite oil in your bag or desk drawer to open and smell when you need a pick me up. Just be careful that it is well sealed. If the concentrated oil spills, it can ruin fabric and create an overwhelming scent in the air.

Essential oils have been used since ancient times for all sorts of ailments, including stomach ache, indigestion, headache and many other things. The power of smell has the ability to cure the body and mind. They can be used only to smell, as part of a topical product like lotion, or taken orally. Be careful and do your research before using, because if taken wrong, especially orally, the concentrated doses can make you sick. It is important to consult with your health care provider before taking anything orally.

CONCLUSION

Thank you for making it through to the end of this book, let's hope it was informative and able to provide you with all of the tools you need to achieve your goals whatever they may be.

The next step is to start trying some of these techniques in your life, and find out what works best for you.

Finally, if you found this book useful in anyway, a review on Amazon is always appreciated!

MINDFULNESS MEDITATION FOR SELF-HEALING

Beginner's Meditation Guide to Eliminate Stress and Anxiety, and Find Inner Peace and Happiness

Sarah Rowland

INTRODUCTION

Congratulations on downloading *Mindfulness Meditation for Self-Healing: Beginner's Meditation Guide to Eliminate Stress and Anxiety, and Find Inner Peace and Happiness*, and thank you for doing so. By picking up this book you are already well on your way to living in the moment more fully than you have ever thought possible and in so doing improve the quality of your life in a wide variety of different ways, some of which are sure to surprise you.

In order to help you along on your path to enlightenment, the following chapters will discuss everything you need to know to get started practicing mindfulness meditation, not just in a quiet place that is free from distractions, but at virtually any point throughout the day, no matter how hectic or stressful the situation might seem at first glance. First you will learn all about the history of mindfulness meditation as it has been practiced throughout the ages before next learning about the basics of the practice and how you can use it to become connected to the present in a deep and meaningful way.

From there you will then learn how to take advantage of the benefits that mindfulness meditation provides during your daily commute, while you are utilizing public transportation, while you are at work and while you are at home going about your daily routine. Finally, you will learn several tips and tricks that are sure to make the process of getting mindful as quick and painless as possible.

There are plenty of books on this subject on the market, thanks again for choosing this one! Every effort was made to ensure it is full of as much useful information as possible, please enjoy!

CHAPTER 1

Understanding Mindfulness Meditation

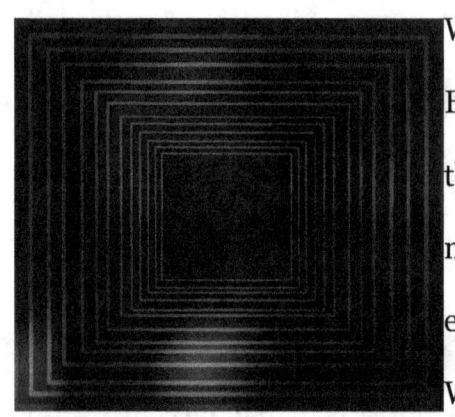

While it has been a part of the Buddhist faith for more than two thousand years, mindfulness meditation has become exceedingly popular in the Western world over the past several decades thanks to its proven ability to improve mental health including the treatment of stress, anxiety and even drug addiction. Professor Jon Kabat-Zinn brought the process to the attention of the modern world in the 1970s by publishing findings that linked it to stress reduction. This, in turn, lead to a flurry of new interest in the practice and a new understanding of the myriad of different ways that being mindful can help improve one's health by directly combating numerous different ailments. Studies on the topic have even proven so conclusive that it is now common to see mindfulness meditation being practiced everywhere from hospitals to prisons to veteran associations.

Since its inception, mindfulness meditation been proven via scientific study to improve the physical wellbeing of those that practice it on a regular basis. At its heart, mindfulness meditation is all about focusing your mind to ensure that you are as fully aware of each moment as fully as possible. This, in turn, allows you to exist more completely in any given moment by expanding your consciousness to the fullest.

While it might sound like a tall order at first, the truth of the matter is that being mindful is a skill which means it can be improved by regular practice in much the same way as any other skill. Luckily, practicing mindfulness meditation is as easy as finding a few moments to focus solely on the present and the information that your senses are providing you in the moment. In fact, if you can find just fifteen minutes a day to practice, you will soon find that your overall stress is likely to decrease and your sense of self is likely to be at an all-time high. This isn't just an ephemeral feeling either, neuroimaging performed on those who practice mindfulness meditation on a regular basis shows that their minds actually process information more effectively, they are able to more easily regulate their emotions and their attention spans than those who do not make the practice a part of their daily routine.

Furthermore, the sooner you begin practicing mindfulness meditation, the greater the chance that doing so will ensure your brain retains more volume as you age, dramatically improving overall brain health as a result. This increased vitality also reaches the hippocampus which, in turn, makes it easier to learn and retain new information with minimal effort. At the same time, the amygdala becomes less active which means that the amount of fear, stress and anxiety that you experience will be decreased as well. Additionally, a daily dose of mindfulness meditation is enough to reduce the amount of cortisol, a hormone that increases stress levels, that the body naturally produces.

In addition to the physical changes that you are likely to experience when meditating regularly, regularly practicing mindfulness meditation will also help you to more easily free your mind from any negative thought patterns you might otherwise find yourself getting stuck on making it easier to focus on the positive instead. Mindfulness meditation is so effective at this task that a recent study out of Johns Hopkins University actually found that it is just as effective at treating anxiety, depression and attention deficit disorder as many of the leading medications specifically designed to do the same thing. Another recent study also showed students preparing to take the Graduate Records Examination, the most common test to obtain admission into graduate school, who practiced mindfulness meditation regularly prior to testing scored approximately 10 percent better than their less mindful peers.

With so many physical and mental benefits, is it any wonder that mindfulness meditation is revered by Buddhists all around the world? The practice has its roots in a type of structured meditation called vipassana which, when translated, refers to a mental state that promotes living in the moment while still being aware of how the present and the future intertwine. Those who master vipassana are said to more fully understand the universe as a whole as well as their place in it.

In order to reach a state of vipassana, practitioners strive for what are known as the three marks of existence: impermanence, non-self and dissatisfaction, which together are believed to bring unity to all living things. Non-self refers to the idea of understanding the boundaries between the self and the physical world with the understanding that coming to terms with these boundaries make it easier to fully grasp the intricacies of both. Meanwhile, dissatisfaction refers to the innate desire seek satisfaction from fleeting experiences and the inevitable feeling that losing these things creates. This leads into the idea of importance as only by accepting the temporary nature of life can true happiness and inner peace be found.

Other reasons to practice mindfulness meditation

- Mindfulness meditation naturally leads to a deeper understanding of the self and allows many people to take stock of their strengths and weaknesses, leading to personal growth.

- Studies show that those who practice mindfulness regularly have a stronger memory, leading to an easier retention of facts in both the long and the short term.

- In addition to the specifics, mindfulness meditation improves overall physical wellbeing with those who practice regularly reporting fewer instances of illness and a more rapid recovery when they do fall ill.

- Mindfulness meditation can help improve emotional control while at the same time increasing one's threshold for pain.

- As surprising as it might seem, making a habit of being mindful can actually make even the most middling music seem more engaging. This deeper level of engagement leads to a general increase of enjoyment, regardless of the type of music or any previous musical preferences.

- With a regular dose of mindfulness meditation, many people experience a dramatic increase in their ability to empathize with others no matter what the situation. Furthermore, it allows practitioners to listen to other viewpoints more actively, more compassionately and results in their ability to withhold judgement on thoughts and ideas that differ from their own.

CHAPTER 2
Mindfulness Meditation Basics

While looking inside yourself with the idea of finding an untapped well of inner peace and tranquility might seem daunting at first, rest assured that it is something anyone can achieve if they dedicate time and mental energy to practice mindfulness meditation every day. What's more, after you get the basics down you will find that almost any situation easily lends itself to being mindful if you simply commit yourself to being fully present in the moment and open yourself completely to the signals that your body is sending you.

While one of the best things about mindfulness meditation is its malleable nature, when you are first getting started it is recommended that you set some time aside each day to specifically devote to the practice. Ideally, this should be someplace that is quiet and during a period of time when you feel relaxed and where you can devote as much as thirty minutes to going deep within yourself without fear of worldly distractions. Remember, being mindful is all about creating space between the sensory information that your body is always sending to your mind and your reactions to that information so the less stimuli you have to deal with at the start, the easier you will find the practice to be.

Getting started

1. *Choose a set time and stick to it:* As with any burgeoning habit, it is important that you create a routine for your mindfulness meditation and stay with it if you hope for the practice to stick. It typically takes 30 days for a new habit to take root in your daily schedule which is why it is important to commit fully to practicing mindfulness meditation if you ever want it to become part of your routine. Due to its low impact nature, nothing external is required, it is very easy for many people to make excuses to get out of meditating, especially if their daily schedule is already filled to bursting.

If you find yourself always coming up with an excuse to get out of meditating in the moment, you may find the following piece of advice particularly useful. "Practice mindfulness meditation for fifteen minutes every day unless, of course, you are extremely busy in which case you should practice for thirty minutes instead." Don't let the outside world intrude on your potential for inner peace, find a time each day that works for you and stick with it no matter what; in a month's time, you will be glad you did.

2. *Get started by focusing on the moment:* While the ultimate goal of mindfulness meditation is to quiet the mind in an effort to find a state of internal calm despite the hustle and bustle of the outside world, many people find it difficult to achieve this state right out of the gate. Instead, you will likely find it easier to start to supplant any thoughts you might have by focusing all of your attention on the signals that your senses are relaying to

you to the exclusion of everything else. While you might not feel as though you are receiving much data on the physical world, especially if you are practicing in a quiet, temperate space, the truth of the matter is that your brain naturally filters out approximately eighty percent of everything it receives, you just need to get in the habit of tapping into it.

With practice, you will learn to tune out your more common thoughts and to instead tune into what is going on around you. When you do this, it is important to simply take in the information your senses are providing without thinking about it too deeply or passing judgement on what you perceive. Judging tends to lead to additional thoughts or, even worse, comparison of the present group of situations to those of the past which is more likely to pull you out of the moment and make finding the state of calm you are looking for even more difficult than it is likely to be, especially when you are just getting started.

Remember, the goal with mindfulness meditation is to get as close to existing in the moment as possible and ignoring everything outside of your current surroundings as much as possible. To reach the required state you are going to want to start by focusing on your breathing, the feel of the air slowly entering and exiting your lungs as well as any smells or tastes that go along with this practice. From there you can then expand the sphere of observation to any other sensations that your body might be experiencing, all the while going deeper into yourself in search of the point where your mind ceases to form new thoughts and simply exists in a state of peaceful relaxation.

3. *Make an effort to avoid judging what you feel:* When you first begin practicing mindfulness meditation it is perfectly natural for your mind to intrude with thoughts about your current surroundings or to fill the void you are trying to achieve with a constant stream of consciousness. This occurs because over the years you

have trained your brain to constantly be moving from one thought to the next in a rush to reach some conclusion or another.

When you find these errant thoughts breaching your sense of mental calm it is important to not interact with them as much as possible and instead to let them simply float away without interacting with them. If you find yourself getting sidetracked it is important to not attach a judgment to what has happened and to instead simply center yourself once more and continue as before. While this step is the most difficult for many people, it is important to keep it up until it becomes second nature as any interaction with the stray thoughts, even if it is just to chastise yourself for getting off track is an easy way to let even more thoughts through which will make it more difficult to find the state of mind that you are looking for.

4. *Keep at it:* When you first begin practicing mindfulness meditation it is important to do so with the right level of expectations regarding your results. Specifically, you will want to keep in mind that your mind is likely to

wander frequently and that you will need to persevere through these periods if you are ever going to reach the level of mental quiet that you are looking for. To understand the ultimate mindset that you are striving for, you may find it helpful to consider the period of blankness the mind enters after a question has been asked but before the answer comes to you. Finding a way to reach this type of state is key to your long-term success.

When it comes to clearing the mind, some people find it helpful to visualize their thoughts as a stream of bubbles that they are watching flow past them; others visualize a gate coming down to block out the stream of consciousness entirely leaving the thoughts to pile up on the far side. While these visualizations can make it easier to be aware of stray thoughts without interacting with them it is important to not become too reliant on them as they are still thoughts and you ultimately want to do away with them once your mind has gotten used to the idea that it doesn't need to constantly be moving from one thought or another. However you manage it, it is important to not to worry about chastising yourself when stray thoughts do emerge and to instead simply acknowledge the lapse and then get back to what you were doing.

What to expect

While many of the benefits of mindfulness meditation include physical changes to the body, it can be difficult to track them without scientific or medical help. Instead, the first positive changes that you are going to likely notice are going to include changes to the mental conditioning you have been subjected too for your entire life. Living in a modern society typically leads to a desire to hide our flaws from others as well as ourselves and to treat uncomfortable thoughts and feelings in much the same way. This, in turn, leads to a desire to revise the truth and rewrite personal histories until they show things in a more flattering light. While not necessarily the most healthy way to handle issues, this common cultural habit is actually an offshoot of the instinctual primal desire towards flight or fight that help ancient humans avoid threats whether they were real or imaginary.

While it was this impulse that helped our ancient ancestors survive and thrive amongst harsh natural conditions, these days it is easy for it to instead lead to an undermining of the very traits and qualities that make us unique. This is perhaps mindfulness meditation's greatest benefit, it allows people to gain a deeper understanding of themselves which is the first step to a greater acceptance of both strengths and weakness and finding the best way to reconcile the two.

In place of this negative and potentially harmful mindset, regularly practicing mindfulness meditation can lead you to what is known as radical acceptance. Essentially it allows you to be more in touch with what you are experience and feeling in the moment without any of the negative filters imposed by society. Radical acceptance allows you to understand that just because you have the occasional negative thought or feeling doesn't mean that there is anything wrong with you and it is an amazing, and free experience. A major part of radical acceptance is embracing all of your firsthand experiences as they really are, something that learning to exist in the moment will make much easier than it otherwise might be. Additionally, you will find that you will soon have a greater tolerance for negative experiences, until you are ultimately able to let them occur without letting them impact your overall mental state.

This improved mental state comes as a natural side effect of learning to be nonjudgmental not just of your thoughts but your experience as well. Cultivating mindfulness means leaning heavily on the suspension of inner judgement which is a result of putting greater thought into your feelings, thoughts and reactions and why they make you feel the way they do.

Additionally, you will likely find that regularly practicing mindfulness meditation naturally improves your ability to be aware of your surroundings at all times, even when you feel otherwise occupied by specific thoughts or problems that you may be facing. Typically, most people are so focused on the mistakes they have made in the past or their plans for the future that they don't have any mental energy left over for the present. This is a precarious situation as it then becomes easy to miss out on all the pleasures of the present without even realizing what it is you are giving up in order to focus on the past which you cannot change or the future which is largely uncertain. Instead of existing in this mental fugue state, existing more frequently in the present allows you to strengthen your awareness of what is happening at any given moment, letting you take charge of your future in a more active way and banishing the specter of missed opportunities that so frequently hangs over the past.

This practice is what is known as meta-awareness which is a state where you are able to interact with your thoughts and feelings in a more objective and detached way. This, in turn, allows you to more accurately measure your experiences to determine how they are affecting your sense of self without the baggage that such things typically carry around with them. Essentially, meta-awareness allows you to view yourself in a detached and objective manner which can benefit virtually every aspect of your life.

CHAPTER 3

Mindfulness During Your Commute

If you are like most people then it is likely that you spend an hour, if not more, of your day commuting to and from work. Most people fill this time by listening to podcasts, cursing at their fellow commuters, catching a quick bite to eat, or, if they are less safety conscious, reading or shaving. While all of these things certainly help pass the time, they do little for their peace of mind or overall wellbeing. That's where practicing mindfulness meditation during the commute comes in as the repetitive nature of the drive is a perfect time to clear your mind and focus on achieving a state of mindfulness that will put other drivers to shame.

By practicing mindfulness meditation on the road, you will find that you arrive at work ready to meet the challenges of the day head on, and arrive home at the end of the day with a clear head and heart, with the cares of the day left somewhere on the turnpike. Practicing mindfulness meditation on the go will allow you to reach your destination in a calm and focused state, that allows the stresses of rush hour traffic to fade into the background. What's more, practicing mindfulness meditation will also ensure you drive as safely as possible because you will be completely focused on the moment and the traffic that surrounds you.

Morning Commute

In order to make the most of your commute you are going to want to practice mindfulness from the very first moment that you enter your vehicle. As such, the first thing that you will want to do is to announce your intention aloud to the universe to help you get into the right mindset from the start. With your intentions made plain, the next thing that you are going to want to do (even before starting your vehicle) is to take several deep breaths. This will allow you to focus your attention on the sensations that your senses are providing you in order to ensure that you are in the right mindset even before you hit the road.

During this period, you want to take special care to focus on your body and the way it feels as you sit in your seat, the way your hands feel on the steering wheel and the way the world around you looks as you stare out at it from behind the windshield. From there, let the sensations of feeling expand outward and downward so that you feel your feet and the pressure you exert on the pedals before starting your vehicle.

As you begin your commute you are going to want to pay special attention to everything that is going on around you, both to the vehicles that you are directly interacting with as well as the people on the sidewalk and the buildings and signs that you previously passed without giving them a second thought. While this is going on be sure to also give some attention to your eyes as they are taking everything in and your ears as they convey the sounds of hundreds, if not thousands, of other people all moving together in relative harmony. Focus on these things, and only these things while you drive and you will be surprised at how much less of a hassle waiting in traffic suddenly becomes.

While this might initially strike you as too simple in order to produce the type of results you are looking for, it is important to put your doubts aside and give it a try before writing it off completely. Remember, when you first get started, even if you have already begun practicing mindfulness meditation in other facets of your life, it is perfectly natural for a stream of thoughts to be running through your head. This is especially true when heading into work as there are likely more  things that you need to do than there are hours in the day to do them. Nevertheless, it is important to put everything else aside and strive to remain in the moment as thoroughly as possible.

For most people, the work day is a time for constant multitasking and this typically begins before the day itself does in the form of one form of electronic communication or another. As such, if you find that you are having a hard time focusing on the task at hand during your commute it may help to make a conscious effort to limit your electronic communication to a set period of time in the morning and ignore it for the rest of your morning until you have reached your destination and are ready to shift your day into high gear. While it may be difficult to ignore all of your notifications at first, after a few weeks you will wonder how you ever functioned when you were so closely tethered to your smartphone.

Suggestions to improve your morning commute
- If you find it hard to get into the right mindset when the time comes to set off for work, consider working a few moments of mindfulness into your day as soon as you wake up. Use the first few moments of the day to stretch your senses, as it were, and try and take in as much information about your surroundings as possible.

Additionally, you may find it useful to take stock of the thoughts that are already running through your mind at this hour and consider how they may affect your morning both for good and for ill. Getting into the habit of running a pre-assessment will allow you to jump into the more productive aspects of mindfulness meditation as soon as you get in your vehicle.

- When you find yourself thinking negative thoughts about the upcoming work day you may find it helpful to avoid banishing them as soon as they appear. Instead, you may want to try cognitively reframing whatever it is that you are thinking of in an effort to turn them around until you can view them in a more positive light. Not only will this help to make each day a little brighter, it will help you approach the day more confidentially and with prevent extra stress or anxiety from clouding your day before it even properly begins.

- Use every moment of gridlock and every red light as a moment to quickly close your eyes, take a deep breath and to refocus on the task at hand. The frequent stop-and-go creates a natural barrier for thoughts that may have slipped through your mental blockade and will help to ensure that you stay on task no matter what else may have grabbed your attention. Remember, your goal during this time is to focus on what your senses are telling you to the exclusion of all else.

- In order to ensure that your morning commute mindfulness session proceeds as smoothly as possible you are going to want to avoid thinking about work as much as possible, especially if something is going on that seems to naturally draw your attention. The pressures of the day can begin naturally building without you even realizing it, leaving you feeling beaten and worn down before the day even starts. Only by remaining vigilant can you stay focused on the moment in order to ensure that your day is ultimately as productive as possible. Taking the time to worry about problems that you can't solve until you get to work will gain you nothing and only make it more difficult for you to focus on the moment.

Evening Commute

While the goal of the morning mindfulness meditation commute is to focus your energy for the coming day, the goal of the afternoon mindfulness meditation commute is to provide you with an opportunity to relax and detox from the stress of the day to ensure that when you make it home your heart is light and your head is clear. When done properly it will ensure that the stress of the day has melted away entirely and that you are ready for whatever it is that the evening may throw at you. With enough practice, instead of dreading the evening commute and the barrier it represents between you and your free time, your evening commute will become a buffer between your happiness and the stresses of the outside world. Remember, practice makes perfect!

Once you reach your vehicle, the first thing that you are going to want to do is to take an extra moment or two to think about the day that is coming to an end and any particular sticking points that may have unpleasant ramifications for the future. Consider why these incidents are sticking in out in your mind and what emotions they have attached themselves to and how you may be able to turn things around tomorrow. With your mental inventory complete, you will them want to make a conscious effort to let all of the negative emotions that you are holding on to float away on the mental breeze. While clearing your head you are also going to want to make a conscious effort to relax, starting with your neck and working your way down your entire body.

Next you are going to want to slowly take several deep breaths. As you do so you are going to want to focus on the feeling of the air as it enters your lungs, filling them until they are full to bursting. As you exhale you are going to want to visualize any stress you may have picked up throughout the day leaving your body as you do so. Visualize the air circulating through your body and consider how the motion makes you feel, use this practice as a gateway to considering the rest of your body and get back in touch with the sensations that the workday may have otherwise dulled. Focus on each of your senses in turn and let them bring you more fully into the moment piece by piece.

Once you have returned to a state of mindfulness, feel the pressure of the seat on your person, the feel of your hands on the steering wheel and the pressure exerted by your foot (or feet) on the pedals. As you drive you are going to want to remain in the moment as completely as possible, blocking out any thoughts that may still linger relating to the workday that you have not yet managed to shake.

However, when you find yourself stopped in traffic or waiting for a red light, instead of refocusing on the task at hand you are going to want to instead focus on the tension that the day has left in your body and focus exclusively on letting go of it and helping your body to relax. Each time you come to a stop you will want to focus on a different part of your body that you can feel holding onto the day's tension and visualize it leaving the body as you begin moving again. Once again you will want to start with your neck and work through your body all the way to the tips of your toes. If you make it through your entire body before you make it home then start again and repeat the process. When you finally reach your destination take an extra moment to consider how much better you feel now than you did before you left work and make one last effort to leave any workday complaints at the office where they belong.

Suggestions to improve your evening commute

- While it is all well and good to try focus on leaving your negative thoughts at the office, it can frequently more difficult in practice than it is in theory. As such, if you find yourself clinging to a particularly negative thought despite your best efforts it is important to push it to the back of your mind instead of letting it drag down your entire commute and prevent you from reaching the state of mindfulness that you are aiming for. Failing to do so will only lead to an excess of tension that you will be unable to get rid of as your body follows your mind's lead. If you simply focus on your breathing and work at remaining in the moment as much as possible, nine times out of ten the thought will pass on its own.

- If you find that you are still unable to get the negative thought or thoughts to subside and allow you to go on your way unmolested, you may find it useful to instead bring the full of your focus to bear on it in an effort to find out just why this thought continues to stick in your mind. In most cases you will find that the thought has actually gathered a greater amount of importance in your mind and that the reality of the situation isn't nearly as bad as your stress, nerves and anxiety have made it out to be.

With a little extra thought, you can often formulate a plan of attack against the negative thought to ensure that when the situation where you actually have to deal with it finally arises you are more than to handle it in the best and most efficient way possible.

- If you are still having trouble letting the day go and regaining the state of mindfulness that you can more easily reach during your morning commute then you might find a mantra to be a good way to get your mind back on the right track. The following are common mindfulness mantras that can be useful in practically any situations:

May I understand my discomfort

May I discard my discomfort

May I be stress free, happy and anxiety free

The cares of the day are behind me

I am in charge of my own happiness

- It is important to keep in mind that there is more than one way to practice mindfulness meditation and that what works for someone else might not work for you. Regardless of what you need to do in order to get into the proper mindset, if it helps you reach a state of mindfulness then it can be considered mindfulness meditation. The only time you need to worry about doing something wrong is if you use the fact that it can sometimes be difficult to find a state of mindfulness as an excuse to give up on the practice completely. Remember, practicing mindfulness is a long journey and it can take several months in order to truly understand yourself, don't get discouraged and keep up the good work.

CHAPTER 4

Mindfulness On The Bus Or Train

If you utilize public transportation you can take the time spent getting where you are going to practice mindfulness meditation as effectively as if you were sequestered peacefully in your own home. There is one caveat however, in order to practice mindfulness meditation effectively it is important that you feel comfortable in the space in which you find yourself. If you find yourself in a situation where something requires your full attention you will likely be unable to reach your full mindfulness meditation potential.

While listening to music while practicing mindfulness meditation in public is not recommended, you may find it helpful to wear headphones as this is a clear signal to those around you that you do not wish to be disturbed. Furthermore, you may find it helpful to set some type of timer as when you get into the zone while being mindful it can be easy to lose track of time.

With the preliminaries out of the way, the first thing that you are going to want to do is to plant your feet firmly a comfortable distance apart from one another whether you are standing or sitting. If standing, take care that you are in a place where you can easily keep your balance. With your feet firmly planted slowly stretch out your body so that you assume the proper posture for your current surroundings. Take a moment to feel your body move with the rhythm of the train/bus and consider how you are connected not just to the transportation you are riding but to all of those who are sharing the journey with you.

Once you feel that you are centered, choose a spot in front of you that is approximately three feet from your current position. Choose a spot that is close to the ground, perhaps just a foot or two above the floor of the bus or train. Slowly lower your eyes to this point on the ground without lowering your neck, it is important to maintain proper posture throughout the exercise. As you feel your eyes begin to dip towards the floor focus exclusively on all of the sensory information they are providing you. From there, slowly incorporate the sensations that are being provided by the rest of your senses.

In order to tune out all of the noise and movement that naturally comes with riding public transportation, focus on your breathing and concentrate on taking rhythmic deep breaths at a nice slow pace. Once you have found a rhythm that works for you consider one of the options below as a means of focusing your attention and attaining a state of mindfulness that might not seem possible otherwise. Remember, practicing mindfulness meditation while using public transportation is even trickier to get the hang of than the other types of mindfulness meditation discussed in these pages. Don't get discouraged if you can't clear your mind as easily as you may be able to elsewhere, as with any other skill practice makes perfect.

Ways to focus your attention

1. Depending on the quality of your ride, you may find that the sensation of movement that you are experiencing to be enough to allow you to focus on the moment. Your body will be constantly moving in this situation, providing you with plenty of sensations to focus on. If

you have to move around during your trip consider focusing on the similarities and differences that the two positions provide you. As you breathe deeply feel the movement coursing beneath your feet, up through your body and all the way to your arms. Use each stop as an opportunity to refocus yourself on the moment. Don't forget to pay enough attention to your other senses that you lose track of your stop!

2. Depending on the quality of your public transportation, you may find that smell is another great anchor to plant you firmly in the present. This is also great practice for taking in sensations without judging them as you are likely to smell plenty of things that are good as well as bad while utilizing public transportation. Rather than making judgement calls regarding particular smells, simply focus on each unique smell as it appears, without breaking out of the rhythm of your breathing.

3. If the public transportation that you are on is particularly raucous, or if you don't have any other way

to keep track of how close you are to your stop, you can count the number of stops you have remaining and repeat the number over and over again in your mind until it forms a type of mantra. This method of keeping in touch with the moment can also be combined with one of the others for maximum effectiveness.

While on one hand, practicing mindfulness meditation while surrounded by so many people can present its own unique challenges, on the other hand it also provides you with a breadth of different sensory information that you are unlikely to get when practicing any other type of mindfulness meditation, including practicing during your commute. Instead of trying to tune everything around you out completely, a more effective choice is to embrace the chaos that surrounds you and use it as a way to drown out any particularly nagging thoughts that have been plaguing you.

Consider the other passengers for example, are they talking to other passengers, ask yourself what they look like, how they act, sound, smell etc. Each stop provides a host of new ways to focus your attention and thus remain in the moment easier. What's more you have more sensations to focus on as well. Focus on the temperature changes as you move along your route as that and any other sensations are likely to change at a moment's notice.

CHAPTER 5

Mindfulness At Work

If asked what the most stressful part of their day is, a vast majority of the population would answer the workday without hesitation and with good reason. The combination of increased responsibility coupled with a lack of control combines to form a perfect storm that naturally leads to high levels of stress, anxiety and tension, often without any relief in sight. Luckily, mindfulness meditation, when practiced discreetly, can not only help mitigate these symptoms, it can also make it easier to focus on a particularly arduous task or project, often leading to unexpected insight and outside of the box thinking. As an added bonus, the state of calm that practicing mindfulness provides, not to mention the boost it will provide to your ability to empathize with others, will surely help to make you extremely popular around the office.

While not possible with all professions, with practice you will find that you can squeeze in a few minutes of mindfulness meditation here and there throughout the day. While the individual efficacy of any particular mindfulness meditation session might be relatively minimal, the overall gestalt will lead to a sense of wellbeing that is greater than the sum of its overall parts. While it might seem difficult to deal with the demands of the day, the demands of your coworkers and everything else that life throws at you, you can consider each micro mindfulness meditation session as islands of calm in an otherwise choppy sea. Mindfulness in the workplace should be thought of as a tool that allows you to squeeze every bit of efficiency out of the workday as long as you think carefully about how to use it as effectively as possible.

If you have already used the period of time prior to arriving at work as an opportunity to practice mindfulness meditation then when you arrive at work you will ideally already be in a state that is primed for making the most of every moment. You can then keep the mindfulness mindset rolling by taking a minute or two between tasks to focus on your breathing and the sensory information that your body is providing you. This doesn't need to be an elaborate process, it can be as quick and as simple as it needs to be. Remember, in this instance quantity definitely trumps quality. Make a point of practicing every day, but if you miss a day, don't use it as an excuse to form unproductive habits, simply pick up where you left off and start again.

Many people find that clearing their minds at work can be exceedingly difficult. If your job leaves you precious little time to sneak in a little mindfulness meditation then your best bet is going to be to start slowly with as little as thirty seconds of mindfulness meditation at a time. With practice, you will be able to sneak in a little mindfulness more frequently until you are ultimately able to string a whole day's worth of micro meditations together with ease.

Types of micro meditation

- For those with office jobs, one of the easiest ways to practice mindfulness meditation at work is by focusing on the sensations that your fingers provide you as you your hands move across the keyboard. Note the rhythmic sound of the keys being pressed and pay special attention to the feeling of your fingers pressing down on each individual key. Consider carefully how your mind forms each word prior to your fingers making it a reality and spend some extra time thinking about the connection between mind and body that is taking place as well as how it is so often taken for granted.

- If you find yourself sitting for most of the day, prior to starting your micro-meditation it is important to consider your posture. Start by relaxing your entire body starting with your neck and working your way down to your toes before reversing the process and starting at the bottom and working your way up. Once you are relaxed focus on the signals that your body is sending you in an effort to pinpoint any areas that are crying out to you in pain. With the problem points identified you are then going to want to adjust your posture until you are completely pain free.

- If you spend a majority of your day responding to emails or various phone notifications then you can simply add thirty seconds between each reply to center yourself and practice mindfulness in its most minute form. While thirty seconds here or there isn't going to do very much good all on its own, the cumulative effect will surprise you. For example, if you respond to eighty requests requiring your response per day then you are actually spending forty minutes of your day being mindful. Give it a try and you will soon realize just how effective this practice can be if you keep it up.

- If your job requires rote repetition then any time you are performing a mundane task you will find that it is an excellent opportunity to practice being mindful. Any activity that mixes physical activity with an ability to only focus on the specifics of what you are doing in a passive way is essentially a free pass to be mindful. All you need to do is focus entirely on the current task and you will be able to easily fill your day with mindful thoughts.

- If your job requires you to constantly interact with coworkers then you can practice mindfulness by simply devoting all of your mental energy to listening to what the other person has to say. While you might not always appreciate your coworkers' insights, giving them the full scope of your attention will allow you to find a state of mindfulness while at the same time allowing them to feel as though you really care about whatever it is that they are saying.

Additionally, this is a good opportunity to practice improving your overall level of empathy as you can use each conversation as an opportunity to try to determine the other person's mindset in an effort to empathize with their position. Remember, the goal here is to focus on the conversation you are having to such an extent that everything else leaves your mind, you won't be able to multitask but others are sure to see your interpersonal skills go through the roof. During these conversations, you are going to want to give some thought to your body language as well, avoid crossing your arms to ensure you appear open to what the other person has to say. You will also want to consider the amount of space between you and the other party as you don't want to interpose any objects between you nor do you want to end the conversation at a distance that is much greater than where you started.

- In order to maximize the effectiveness of your end of the day commute and the mindfulness meditation you are hopefully practicing therein, you should use the last few minutes of the workday to compartmentalize everything that has happened during the time you were hard at work. Consider what you have managed to accomplish, reflect on your successes and your failures in light of the bigger picture and consider what they mean overall for the days to come. With that done, mentally close the door on the workday and remind yourself that any work problems won't need to be solved until tomorrow. Close the book on the workday before you leave your place of business and you will find your next session of mindfulness meditation to be much more effective than it otherwise might be. Above all, repeat the mantra that tomorrow is another day and another opportunity to get everything right.

While it might seem that making an effort to practice mindfulness in the office will lead to an overall decrease in productivity, the reality is that the opposite is true. Especially if you have a particularly hectic job you likely find that you often have to react to things without thinking through all the possible outcomes of your response. With your head cleared from frequent micro-meditations, however, you will find that the moments in which you have to make important decisions naturally seem to expand in order to provide you with all the time you need to make the right choice, right now.

Remember, when you react to something you at taking a nearly automatic action, letting the stimuli that sent you down this path take control of the situation. However, if you respond instead of react then you are making a well-reasoned choice based on all available data. Reasoned responses lead to better solutions every single time.

With enough time spent practicing mindfulness at work, you will also find that you have gained the ability to approach problems both old and new in ways that you had previously never considered. This will only be the case, however, if you stop thinking about incidents that require your attention as problems and instead consider them in the framework of challenges to be overcome. Problems are simply roadblocks to success while challenges, on the other hand, are incidents that can be learned from and bested for the betterment of you and your place of business. When you come across a challenge that has you stumped, consider writing it down and focusing on it completely to the exclusion of everything else. If you have been practicing mindfulness regularly you will be surprised at how quickly a previously unthought of solution may reveal itself.

CHAPTER 6
Mindfulness At Home

There is perhaps no easier place to practice mindfulness than in your own home as it is there that you have the greatest level of control over yourself and your surroundings. In fact, once you get in the habit of practicing mindfulness on a regular basis there will hardly be anything that you can do that won't lend itself to practicing mindfulness with nothing more than a little extra thought and a little more practice. Who knows, the ways you can practice mindfulness in the home may even surprise you.

Practice mindfulness while taking care of everyday chores

Prior to beginning your journey to understand mindfulness meditation you likely considered taking care of your household chores to be the epitome of drudgery and menial labor. Once you look at them through the lens of mindfulness meditation, however you will soon find that they are one of the best opportunities to practice mindfulness meditation while still being outwardly productive to boot. Remember, any activity that has a physical component that doesn't require your full and active attention can easily become an outlet for mindfulness meditation as long as you approach it in the right way.

When it is time to tackle your chores, the first thing that you are going to want to do is to take a few moments before hand to clear your mind and get in touch with the signals that your body is sending you. With your mind primed, dive into the moment to moment nature of the activity you are pursuing with the goal of limiting thought to the extreme. Instead, consider the way your hands feel as they go through the motions of whatever it is you are doing.

Consider the information your eyes are providing you as the task alters the physical world in one way or another as well as the smells that accompany the task and what it is that they signify. Finally, once you are completed take another moment to enjoy the feeling of accomplish that is sure to manifest from a job well done and consider the difference of the before and after nature of the task you just completed. For the best results, prepare everything you need to do for several chores beforehand so that you can string the periods of mindfulness together as much as possible. With practice, you can easily create a state of mindfulness that lasts for an hour, if not more.

Practice mindfulness while you are bathing

It doesn't matter if your bathing habits skew towards the morning or the evening, you can easily use this time to practice mindfulness meditation and either help you get ready to start your day off right or to further decompress when the day is at an end. While most people rush through their daily bath or shower with nary a thought, this period of time is rife with sensations for your body to track while at the same time being devoid of any of the distractions that might plague your mindfulness meditation in other settings.

Before you begin your bathing ritual take an extra moment to center yourself and get in touch with your body. If it is early in the morning make an effort to put off all thoughts of the day ahead and if it is evening push out everything that has happened during the day in an effort to get into the moment as quickly as possible. Once you are ready, start by considering the feel of the water on your skin and how the hot, or cold, water feels engulfing your body completely and running down your skin.

Use the repetitive tasks that you are performing as a gateway to reach a mental state that is free of anything but the sensations you are feeling right now. Smell is also an extremely powerful sense in this instance and focusing on the scents that surround you is also a fantastic way to push out other thoughts as they try to intrude.

Practice mindfulness while exercising

While it might seem surprising, the mindset of the average individual who is exercising is already remarkably similar to the mindset of someone who is practicing mindfulness meditation. This is caused by the fact that exercise automatically pushes the sensations that the body is sending out to the forefront of the mind and the concentration that many types of exercise require in order to see the best results. As such, it then only takes a little push to tip this type of mindset over into mindfulness meditation in its entirety. As an added bonus studies show that those who practice mindfulness while they exercise are known to report an increase in their level of endurance as well as a measurable boost to their overall performance.

The key to pushing the one into the other is to reduce your focus on getting everything you are doing exactly right and to instead focus on the body parts that you are pushing to their limits, how they feel as they move and the sensations they are providing you with as you put them through their paces. Each time you complete an exercise and move onto the next you can use the pause in the forward momentum as an opportunity to refocus your attention on the moment and banish any stray thoughts that may have crept in while your focus was elsewhere.

While you are focusing on the moment it is important to not lose track of what you are doing entirely as you may push yourself too hard and accidentally cause undue strain on your body. With that in mind, it doesn't matter what type of exercise you enjoy or where you perform it, there are likely going to be a whole host of sights, sounds and smells to draw you into the moment as thoroughly as possible. For the best results, start off with a focus on what it is you are doing and let yourself get into a rhythm. From there, let your body take care of itself and use the sensations the exercise provides to push everything else out of your mind so that you can find the sense of inner peace that you are striving for.

Practice being mindful while utilizing social media

Despite the fact that it might seem counterintuitive, if you make a concentrated effort to do so, you can even practice mindfulness meditation while you are utilizing social media of all types. While the siren's call of a social media notification can easily draw you out of the moment during several types of mindfulness meditation, if you allocate a set time with which to check up on what your friends are doing you can actually find a state of mindfulness while doing so.

For this type of mindfulness meditation to work, the first thing that you are going to want to do is to eliminate any other potential distractions before you get to work. This is an extremely crucial step due to the fact that a majority of people check social media sites as a means of multitasking. With any distractions out of the way, you will first want to clear your mind and make an effort to inhabit the moment as much as possible. With the proper mindset obtained you can then look at the pictures or text that relates to your personal history with an eye towards inhabiting those past moments as thoroughly as possible.

For every picture that you see or tweet that you read consider what was taking place at its time of inception. Remember the way you felt at the time and let the memory wash over you completely. Make an effort to put yourself into the time and place in question by remembering the various signals that your body was providing you with at the time. Once you have this in mind, you will then want to go even deeper into the memory by starting with the smells you can remember. If the day was hot or cold, try and conjure up the way the temperature felt on your skin and if it was loud, consider what it is your ears were taking in. With enough practice, you will find that you are able to block out all external stimuli and exist solely in a previous moment.

Practice reflecting on the preceding day in a mindful fashion
Prior to going to bed at the end of the day you may find it helpful to practice mindfulness meditation, especially if you have difficulty falling asleep or staying asleep due to stresses that come up naturally during the day. This process of offloading your stress from the day can be done either by taking a mental inventory, but you may find the process more beneficial if you instead write down what has been troubling you.

As usual, you will want to begin by taking a few moments to center yourself and to work to get into the type of mindset that will make it easier to find a state of mindfulness once you get into the bulk of the exercise. When you get ready to write down what you remember about your day you may find it helpful to write out by hand what you remember rather than typing up a journal as the tactile experience of writing can be an easy way to tie yourself to the moment. Likewise, when you want to go back and read what you have previously written you will have that tactile experience of writing it the first time to reflect on in addition to focusing on what happen in the entry that you are reading.

When you start writing it is important that you take stock of the day as a whole and make an effort to include absolutely everything that happened to you in the past twenty-four hours, regardless of how meaningless it seems at the time. As you write you are going to want to commit yourself to remembering each moment as fully as possible, complete with all of the various stimuli that were taking place as the memory was made. With practice, this detailed examination of your day will make it easier for you to pick out various sensations that you might have missed while practicing other forms of mindfulness meditation.

Once you have a little bit more perspective on the events that have unfolded and read back through what you have written you will often find that the individual moments that seem the most innocuous have the greatest impact on the future. Once you have written enough journal entries to begin to notice this type of pattern you will then be primed to notice all of the little moments more throughout your day and let moments of mindfulness slip in as well.

Practice mindfulness meditation to start your day out right
No matter how rushed you feel you are in the morning, you can find a few minutes to practice mindfulness meditation if you make a concentrated effort to do so. The easiest way to do so is by taking a few extra moments to really savor your favorite morning drink be it coffee, tea or even soda or an energy drink. What's more, if you shower in the mornings as well, you can string together a group of mindfulness meditation sessions practically from the moment you wake up until you reach your workplace. From there, if you do it right you can be mindful throughout your day right up until it is time for bed.

The morning mindfulness meditation session is one of the easiest to get the hang of as the first cup of an energizing beverage of the day is naturally more potent than those that follow it as your body has had all the hours you were asleep to get the caffeine out of your system ensuring that the first jolt is the most powerful that you are going to feel throughout the day. This, in turn, naturally draws you into the present more fully, especially if you take the extra time to really appreciate it. Remember, this may be the only truly relaxing moment of your entire day, it is best to make it count.

For the best results, you are going to want to wake up with the idea of mindfulness on the brain. As you wake in the morning take a few extra moments to consider the thoughts that are already racing through your head and consider why they are there without interacting with them directly. If your thoughts are all about the day ahead, make a concentrated effort to push them aside until you have successfully finished your morning mindfulness meditation routine. If possible, go ahead and slip into a state of mindfulness directly after taking stock of your mental inventory.

Once you are properly adapted to the moment the next thing that you are going to want to do is to pay special attention to the preparation of your drink of choice. While there is certainly going to be more to be aware of if you are grinding coffee beans and filling an espresso machine, even pulling out a teabag or taking a cold drink from the refrigerator has plenty of sensations to offer when it comes to locking you in place in the moment. As you go through the routine of preparation consider the anticipation of what is to come, the smell of the beverage brewing or the feel of the cold can against your skin. Regardless of your drink of choice it is important to really savor the moments before you take your first sip and take in the world around you as much as possible. The goal here is to be able to completely recall the events leading up to your first drink if you are planning to write about it at the end of the day.

Once you are ready to actually take your first drink, you want to find a quiet spot to sit and really appreciate the first sip. Take in the smell of the drink, the smell of it and the feel as it hits your tongue and rolls down your throat. Focus on the feel of the cup or can in your hand and the heat or the cold that is radiating from it. Try and remain in the moment as much as possible and chart the course of the caffeine as it invigorates every part of your body one by one. As you feel the liquid running through your body consider the benefits it is providing you and how it is giving you the energy to face the coming day head on.

During this period, it is important to give the beverage the full sum of your attention, if you find your mind wandering the details of the day simply refocus and bring your mind back to the task at hand. Once you are finished, take note of the way the empty vessel feels now that it is devoid of the precious liquid. Finally, take another few moments to take in the silence around you before readying yourself to start your day in earnest.

Practice dancing or listening to music mindfully

It doesn't matter who you are dancing with or why you are dancing in the first place, dancing itself is an inherently mindful act. Proper dancing requires the complete focus of the dancer both to ensure that the body follows as it should but also of the music, the tempo and the way they work together to affect the body. If you already love to dance, then all you need to do is be aware of the ways in which it helps you be mindful to take full advantage of their effects.

Much like dancing, playing music in such a way that it demands your attention is an inherently mindful action. As long as you take the time to focus on the moment and consider the way your body relates to the creation of each individual note. Consider the other musicians you are playing with and the ways the smallest change in what you are doing can affect the flow of the whole. For those who are not musically inclined, chanting may be a viable alternative. Repeating a phrase or mantra can be an effective way of achieving a higher state of mindfulness. Like with dancing, an understanding of the mindful principles at play will make you more aware of them in the moment.

Practice being mindful with your family

While oftentimes practicing mindfulness meditation means spending time alone, this isn't a prerequisite for practicing successfully. In fact, practicing mindfulness meditation with your family is actually a great way to spend time with your loved ones, as long as you do it properly that is. The best way to go about doing so is to use group meal times to foster a sense of mindfulness with everyone involved. While it might seem difficult to get multiple people to focus on the moment, as long as things are handled properly, and all technology is left outside the kitchen and/or dining room then the process is easier than you might expect.

First things first, you are going to want to get everyone involved in the preparation for the food, you don't need to make a big deal about the mindfulness aspects inherent in the process, all you need to do is simply encourage everyone to give their full attention to their assigned preparation task. Once everyone has settled into the rhythm of food preparation then you will all be on your way to focusing on the moment to the exclusion of all else.

Once the food is prepared, gather everyone around the table and, before anyone takes their first bite, take a few moments to start your deep breathing exercises and consider all of the sensations that the fresh meal is sending to your body. The first few times you try this with your family you will want to point out the sights of the meal that you have prepared as well as the smells that are wafting out from it. Eventually, this will become simply another part of the meal and you won't have to break your own state of mindfulness to ensure that everyone else is following along.

In addition to taking in the preliminary sights and smells of the meal you will want to make eye contact with each member of your family and as you do so contemplate the special connection that you both share thanks to the meal you have helped prepare together and encourage family members to do the same with everyone else. Finally, you will want to audibly express your gratitude that you can all be together right here, right now, in this particular moment in time.

With the preliminary mindfulness meditation out of the way, it will then be time to get to the main event, the consumption of the meal that you have all come together to prepare for one another. Prior to starting you will want to make a point of cautioning your family to avoid eating to rapidly and to instead make an effort to really taste each bite of food you take, and enjoy the sensations it provides.

As you eat you will want to anchor yourself to the moment by considering all of the flavors that the food provides, feel your teeth tear into it and break it down and feel any spices that may be used as they create a physical sensation in your mouth. You will want to picture each bite as it moves into your stomach and consider the various vitamins and nutrients that it is passing on to your body.

If you try hard enough, you should be able to taste the whole of the universe in every bite. Focus on this thought as you eat and consider the joy you feel when receiving the bounty of the universe and sharing it with the people you love. Breaking bread with someone forms a unique bond with that person quite unlike anything else, consider this as you eat and focus on the moment to ensure it lasts as long as possible.

Another good thing about making a habit out of eating mindfully is that it will naturally draw you to meal options that are naturally healthier overall as processed foods that are full of artificial preservatives don't typically require enough preparation to draw in the entire family. Not only will a careful consideration of the food you eat lead you to feel full more quickly than you otherwise will, such a careful consideration of the food will also often make the meal taste more delicious than those meals which are consumed quickly and without a second thought. As you get more in touch with what you are eating you will also find that it is much easier to determine if you are really in need of sustenance or if you are considering eating for some other, less healthy, alternative.

One downside of practicing mindfulness meditation with the entire family is that if one or more members aren't on board, the exercise loses much of its potency. As such, you are going to want to take special care to ensure that everyone is on the same page for the best results. In order to do this, you may want to start by explaining that the food that you are about to eat is a direct gift from the universe at large. By explaining every step that was required for the food to get from where it was created all the way to your table you will add a weight to the meal that is often lost when people are disproportionately disassociated from their food as most people are in this day and age.

While the preparation of the meal and the first few minutes once you all sit down to eat should be relatively quiet, that doesn't mean that the entire meal should be consumed in silence. If this were the case then you would be little better off than eating alone. You will, however, want to make it a point to keep conversation focused on the meal itself. To get the ball rolling you are going to want to foster conversation about the quality of the meal, its nutritional value and the general bounty of what has been provided for you. While you won't always be able to keep the conversation in this sphere, you will want to make a point of avoiding any negative conversation or heated debates as these types of topics will only make it more difficult for everyone to remain mindful throughout the meal.

While eating mindfully will likely make each meal seem as though it lasts longer than you are used to, the reality of the situation is that a mindful meal should last no longer, or be any larger, than a normal meal and may actually even be smaller than the meals that you were eating before as your greater level of concentration will often allow you to eat smaller meals while feeling just as full as you otherwise would.

CHAPTER 8

Tips For Improving Your Ability To Be Mindful

Don't focus on your mind

For many people, especially those who are new to mindfulness meditation, the idea of clearing your mind can be exceedingly confusing if not apparently impossible. This is perfectly understandable, especially as it is very difficult for anyone, even mindfulness experts to clear their minds of absolutely all thoughts. Instead of worry that you are doing something wrong, you will find better success if you simply focus on receiving as much information from your senses as possible and let your mind take care of itself. Remember, as long as you are feeling the benefits of mindfulness meditation there is no single right or wrong way to practice it.

Don't worry about finding the "perfect" position

While there are certainly various positions that make the practice of mindfulness meditation easier than others, there is no one perfect position that is suddenly going to pull you into the moment. Rather than looking for an ideal position that is right for all types of mindfulness meditation, you should focus on finding a position that you can hold for a prolonged period of time that doesn't promote any aches or pains that may ultimately distract you from your true goal. Remember, while you want to choose a position that is relaxing, you also don't want to find one that is so relaxing that it causes you to fall asleep. Work on finding a position that straddles the line somewhere in the middle in order to see the best results.

Ensure you are focusing properly

If you are having a difficult time bringing your consciousness to the moment, the first thing you are going to want to do is to put all of your focus into feeling your breath. If you find that the feeling of air moving in through your nose and out through your mouth isn't enough to keep your mind focused, you may have better luck focusing on what your abdominal muscles instead. As such, instead of focusing on the breath itself, focus on the sensation of breathing in and out that is provided by the muscles in your abdomen expanding and contracting.

Don't get ahead of yourself
With so many different ways to practice being mindful, it can be easy for those who are new to the practice to want to jump straight

into one of the more complicated types of meditation straight out of the gate. Then, when they have trouble achieving a state of mindfulness they get discouraged and give up before they have experienced any of the benefits that meditation can provide. As such, it is best to start off slowly with the basic form of mindfulness meditation and practice existing in the moment when there are no distractions around before moving to a more advanced version of the exercise.

Don't get discouraged when your mind wanders

For many new mindfulness meditation practitioners controlling a wandering mind can seem like an impossible task. This is a perfectly normal feeling and it is important that you work through this early stage with perseverance and hard work if you ever hope to reap the benefits that mindfulness meditation provides. There is no trick to this practice, all it takes is lots of repetition and a commitment to always bringing your mind back into focus as soon as it begins to wander.

Be prepared for intense emotions
While not everyone is going to experience extreme emotions while practicing mindfulness meditation, it is important to be aware of

the potential for doing so in order to be prepared if it does happen to you. Intense feelings of joy are common but, on the other hand, some practitioners have also experienced sudden bouts of anger, fear, grief or depression. The important thing to remember is that these feelings aren't indicative of your overall mental state and that only by focusing on the moment as fully as possible can you prevent them from interrupting your feeling of mindfulness.

Don't focus on the results, focus on the experience
Mindfulness meditation can provide a wide variety of benefits for those that practice it on a regular basis. However, that doesn't mean that you are going to start experiencing everything that mindfulness meditation has to offer as soon as you start. What's worse, practicing with one eye planted firmly in the future will make it much more difficult to exist fully in the moment and, as a result, push any results you might see even further into the future. Focus on getting to a point where you can exist in the moment and let everything else take care of itself.

Don't let negative thoughts fester
One of the greatest impediments to successful mindfulness meditation are negative or stressful thoughts that tend to cloud the

mind and make it difficult to listen to the signals that your body is sending you. As such, for the best results, you are going to want to make a concentrated effort to let go of these types of thoughts before you start meditating otherwise they are likely to draw your focus away from what you should be doing.

Understand the physical changes that your mind is going through
While you are training your brain to be more mindful it is important to understand just what it is you are actually doing and to do that you need to understand the basics of how the brain works. Specifically, habits are formed because neurons move through the brain via the path of least resistance. The more that a given neural pathway is used (by repetition of a given thought or action) the more likely the neurons in the brain are going to use that path in the future. When you make a concentrated effort to be more mindful on a daily basis you are creating new neural pathways and the only way to ensure that they are used regularly is to practice, practice, practice.

Don't worry about a little numbness
In most situations, if you find that your leg or legs have gone to sleep, the most common response is to reposition yourself to

ensure that blood starts flowing to the affected area in a greater quantity. While no one is suggesting that you cut off the blood flow to your limbs completely, if you are only practicing mindfulness meditation for fifteen or thirty minutes at a time then a bit of numbness can be a powerful tool when it comes to helping you focus on the moment. Remember, mindfulness meditation is all about using sensations, all sensations, to anchor yourself in the moment as fully as possible. Don't be too anxious to shut out sensations that you are feeling, even if they are typically considered to be negative.

Handle distractions properly

While you likely won't encounter many distractions when you are practicing mindfulness meditation at home, the greater the variety of places that you practice meditating in, the more likely you are to be interrupted when you are in the middle of connecting to the moment. When this occurs, it is important to treat the distraction as you would any other errant thought and simply let it float away until you can continue whatever it was you were doing. While often easier said than done, it is important to approach distractions in this fashion as otherwise you are likely to let your emotions get the best of you and once that happens it will be even more difficult to get back into the state that you were in before the distraction first brought itself to your attention.

Take care to avoid drowsiness

It is perfectly natural for the process of mindfulness meditation to lead to a feeling of drowsiness, especially if you are practicing at the end of a long day. If you hope to get the most out of the practice you are going to want to avoid this feeling as much as possible which may mean taking extra precautions before you get started. Specifically, you are going to want to avoid eating heavy meals before you begin your mindfulness meditation practice or exercising to the point of exhaustion. If you still find yourself becoming drowsy, turn the focus of your mind from the body to the mind itself and try and probe the edges of your mind in an effort to determine just what sensations being drowsy provides. If, after fifteen minutes or so, if the feeling persists you may want to find something else to do for a time until the feeling passes.

Don't seek comparison with others

While the basic practice of mindfulness meditation is relatively universal, the end results from practicing on a regular basis are going to be dramatically different for everyone who gives mindfulness a serious try. As such, rather than wasting your time comparing your results to the results of others, you will have a more productive experience if you focus all of that curious energy and double down on your own mindfulness meditation practice. If you are trying to analyze what you are trying to do, or what you are potentially doing wrong, then you are not going to be truly in the moment and the results you are looking for will be forever out of reach. Rather, you will note better results in the long run if you choose to simply meditate as effectively as you can and trust that the practice will lead to the types of results that you are looking for.

CONCLUSION

Thank for making it through to the end of *Mindfulness Meditation for Self-Healing: Beginner's Meditation Guide to Eliminate Stress and Anxiety, and Find Inner Peace and Happiness*, let's hope it was informative and able to provide you with all of the tools you need to achieve your goals relating to mindfulness meditation whether it is something that you are interested in doing just once in a while or if you are hoping to reach a point where a majority of each and every day is spent being as fully committed to being focused on the present as humanly possible. Just because you've finished this book doesn't mean there is nothing left to learn on the topic, expanding your horizons is the only way to find the mastery you seek.

The next step is to stop reading and to get started practicing mindfulness meditation as frequently as possible. While initially you may not feel as though you are getting very much out of the time that you put in, the more you keep at it the more quickly the positive benefits of being mindful are going to start stacking up. Don't get discouraged if at first you find that your mind remains unruly, every moment you spend fully engrossed in the moment will make it easier to reach the desired mental state in the future. Take it one step at a time and you will soon find yourself fully engaged in the present without even trying.

There are so many different types of mindfulness meditation that, as long as you keep at it, you are bound to find something that works for you sooner or later. The only way that you won't be able to get anything out of mindfulness meditation is if you give up before you have tried them all. Remember, it takes at least thirty days for a new routine to become habit, and practice makes perfect!

Finally, if you found this book useful in anyway, a review on Amazon is always appreciated!

YOU'RE ALL YOU NEED

Real Happiness Through The Power of Meditation

Sarah Rowland

INTRODUCTION

Congratulations on downloading this book and thank you for doing so.

The following chapters will discuss Meditation and the various ways to practice Meditation in your life.

There are plenty of books on this subject on the market, thanks again for choosing this one! Every effort was made to ensure it is full of as much useful information as possible, please enjoy!

CHAPTER 1
What Is Meditation?

Ask anyone around you what meditation is and they"ll most likely come with answers such as it is a prayer or some form of worship or mental concentration. If meditation can be powerfully summed up in a few words – it is a way of life. Meditation is absolute awareness of the present. Anything you do with keen awareness and focus is meditation. Mindful walking or concentrating on your breath can also be meditation. Listening to the sound of hustling trees, a gushing waterfall or birds chirping in your backyard is also meditation. When you direct you consciousness to any activity or object around you without any distraction, you are practicing meditation.

Contrary to popular misconception, meditation is not a method but simply a way of life. Meditation is a lifestyle. It is a state of being when the mind is liberated from all its chaotic thoughts to focus on the present. It is nourishment for your soul. It celebrates universal value such as kindness, sharing, nonviolence, peace, responsibility and more. In an era where humanity and the world around us is quickly fragmenting, meditation guides us towards a peaceful path. The term is used inaccurately and freely in the contemporary world, which is why there is a sense of ambiguity associated with it. Some people use the term meditation for contemplation or the process of thinking. Others go a step further and think meditation is all about day dreaming or visually fantasizing. Meditation can be any of these. However at its core, it is attaining a restful mind. Meditation is not religion. It is a spiritual science that encapsulates discipline, well-defined principles and verifiable results.

To reach the perfect state of meditation, we require focus instead of a scattered mind and clarity in place of dullness. There has to be an increasing keenness to observe our thoughts and state of mind instead of being clouded by emotions or prejudice. Meditation will train you to be honest to yourself rather than playing deception games and walking free from unpleasant problems. You need endless reserves of patience since you won"t become an overnight Zen master. Operating from a level of self-acceptance, self-assuredness, confidence, energy and enthusiasm brings more peace to the mind. Balance and harmony are the most popular meditation buzzwords. It is all about achieving a state of balance or harmony with your physical, mental and spiritual faculties.

A Tibetan Lama was closely monitored by a brain scan machine to examine physiological functions during a deep state of meditation. The scientist helming the experiment said, "Very well Sir. The machine reveals that your brain can slip into a deep

state of relaxation. It validates your practice." "No", replied the Lama, pointing to his brain, "This validates your machine."

The word meditation originates from two Latin terms: mediatari (which means to think or dwell upon) and mederi (which means to heal). The Sanskrit derivative „medha" implies wisdom.

Meditation is a wonderful means or transforming the body, mind and spirit. A disciplined and consistent meditation practice has several benefits, including enhanced concentration, calmness, positivity and clarity. Meditation has the ability to transform your thought patterns and mental habits to cultivate a newer and more positive way of being. With dedicated practice, you nurture a profoundly serene and energized mind state. These experiences have a completely transformational effect, and can lead to a newer level of understanding lie.

The basic objective of meditation is spiritual renewal and to achieve a state of absolute peace. Meditation helps expand the practitioner"s realm of conscious to enable them to let go of the physiological rigidity of attachments. You learn to move above the pettiness of ego, insecurity, vanity and snobbery. There is a greater sense of elevation and unison with a strong spiritual force that endows us with emotional maturity.

The history of meditative practice is closely interwoven into a religious context within cultures that subscribed to its philosophy. Some of the most ancient meditation references can be traced back to the Vedas of Hindu religion prevalent in India and Nepal. Around 6th or 5th centuries BCE, other types of meditation such as Confucianism and Taoism evolved in China, in addition to a variety of practices that developed in Hinduism, Buddhism and Jainism in India and Nepal.

In the west the seed of meditation was planted in 20 BCE, when Philo of Alexandria wrote about some kind of spiritual exercises marked by concentration and attention. Plotinus took the theory further in the 3rd century to develop full-fledged meditation techniques.

There are a staggering variety of meditation techniques since the practice is highly personal. Some practices such as mindful meditation and focused attention are heavily rooted in scientific research. The focus can be on anything from breathing to a bodily sensation to a specific external object. One of the core aspects of meditation is to singularly focus on a single point or objects, and draw attention to this focal point when the mind starts wandering. Meditation harbors several misunderstandings, including the notion that one must cease to think while meditating. While silencing the distracting noise originating in the mind is valid, there"s no way you can stop thinking completely. The objective is not to stop thinking but cultivation of clearer insights by drowning out the pointless noise that stems from within, using discrimination. You don"t need to stop thinking. You only need to halt compulsive, robotic, unintelligent mental activities that induce fatigue, are generally pointless and sometimes, downright dangerous.

Ajahn Chah, an influential Buddhadhamma teacher said, ""Try to be mindful, and let things take their natural course. Then your mind will become still in any surroundings, like a clear forest pool. All kinds of wonderful, rare animals will come to drink at the pool, and you will clearly see the nature of all things. But you will be still. This is the happiness of the Buddha."

Meditation is actually a three way process that that involves a powerful state of consciousness brining clarity, calmness and bliss. The first step is about receiving sensory stimuli and reacting in more uncontrolled manner. It is about bouncing from thought to thought by following different physical and psychological reactions. The same thought or stimulus can bring about different reactions at various times. For example, we may spot a dog and feel nostalgic about a cute pet we once had and loved. It triggers a comforting and warm feeling in us, where we achieve a state of relaxation. In a different situation we may start fearing the dog, thinking it may start attacking us and develop thoughts of paranoia, feeling more fearful and physically rigid.

It is commonly accepted fact that focusing your thinking on a single behavior can transform your habits. For instance, athletes who constantly visualize playing successfully end up advancing their game considerably. Meditation is also about saying and doing things that drive our subconscious mind towards your goals. It can be harnessed in multiple ways provided you have the power to recognize its benefits.

CHAPTER 2

43 Spectacular Benefits Of Meditation

We all know by now that meditation is good for us. How exactly though? There have been innumerable studies and extensive research projects to explore the impact of meditation in everyday life. Want some reasons to kick-start a solid meditation practice. We take you through the powerful benefits of a dedicated, consistent and disciplined meditation lifestyle.

1. Meditation enhances the flow of air into our lungs, thus making breathing easier.
2. It lowers your heart rate and boosts blood flow within the body.
3. Meditation reduces chronic illnesses such as arthritis and allergies.
4. A regular and consistent meditation practice improves your overall immunity.
5. Meditation assists in weight loss.
6. It prolongs the process of aging to give you a fresher, more youthful and rejuvenated appearance.

7. Meditation is highly effective for combating headaches and migraine.
8. It boosts your athletic performance.
9. Meditation is great for fighting stress induced infertility.
10. It builds high levels of self confidence and self esteem.
11. Meditation enhances creativity and productivity.
12. It increases the practitioner"'s ability to solve complicated problems.
13. Meditation awards the practitioner with greater emotional stability.
14. It gives you the vision to see the larger perspective in any situation.
15. Meditation enhances your memory power and learning abilities.
16. Meditation increases self-awareness, acceptance and happiness.
17. A regular meditation practice reduces depression and other mental ailments.
18. Meditation reduces pre and post partum depression in women.

19. It boosts the concentration of the brain's grey matter, thus enhancing our cognitive abilities.
20. Meditation helps you live in the present and develop a deep sense of gratitude and appreciation for it.
21. It helps in quitting smoking, alcohol and other addictions.
22. Meditation helps you sleep better
23. It reduces your aggression level.
24. A regular meditation practice diminishes anxiety and restless thoughts.
25. Meditation helps in making sounder decisions and more accurate judgments.
26. It awards you the calmness to act in productive and considerate manner.

27. Reduces dependency on pills and drugs.

28. Meditation helps you develop a higher sense of intuition.

29. It assists in creating sexual desire and energy.

30. Meditation is an excellent way for curing phobias and deep seated fears.

31. It facilitates better communication between the brain''s left and right hemisphere.

32. Meditation helps you experiences a profound sense of assurance.

33. Regular meditation practitioners experience a lesser need for medical care.

34. Meditation helps decrease muscle tension.

35. A consistent and disciplined meditation practice is wonderful for developing will-power.

36. Meditation offers a greater sense of inner-directedness.

37. It increases compassion and empathy for other beings.

38. A consistent meditation practice lowers cholesterol levels, thus lowering the risk of heart diseases.

39. Meditation provides substantial relief to asthma patients.

40. It keeps the body"s hormones well balanced to award practitioners a more radiant and beautiful skin.

41. Meditation acts as a effective recovery mechanism for food related addiction such as binge eating.

42. Meditation enhances your sense of focus and concentration.

43. Meditation is excellent for countering grief after the loss of a loved one.

CHAPTER 3

Types Of Meditation – Pick The One That Works For You.

Straight off, there"s no good, bad, better or „more effective than the other" meditation technique. There are several techniques and all are wonderful, depending on what exactly you are seeking though a meditative practice. For instance, if you are looking for a more stress-free that comprises living in the present than worrying about the future, mindful meditation can work wonders. Similarly, if your idea is to fulfill a goal through meditation, visualization can be a highly potent technique. We bring you a treasure trove of different types of meditation to help you decide the one that works best for you.

Guided Visualization – Guided visualization is a relatively new technique that aims to offer enhanced personal development and goal achievement. The premise on which it is based is, "we become what we think." The focus is on setting clear goals and meditating while visualizing the goal in order to fulfill it. Practitioners visualize their goal in a relaxed and positive manner by imagining themselves in a desirable situation. A guide or master conducts the entire meditation through the process of a powerful narration that takes you through circumstances that you wish to manifest through the process.

Beginners commence their guided visualization practice with an instructor

Mindfulness – Mindful meditation is another popular meditation form that hails from the Buddhist tradition. This technique is all about being fully immersed in your present, and observing your thoughts in a non-judgmental manner. It is acknowledging the present, allowing the mind to stray, accepting any thoughts that arise, and being fully aware of the present. The practice comprises sitting crossed legged and focusing attention completely on the breath. When wandering thoughts take over, the practitioner simply acknowledges them, and gently returns focus back to the breath or object. Research has strongly pointed out to the fact that a disciplined and consistent mindfulness practice reduces stress, overcomes depression and combats distress.

In the east, mindful meditation is often referred to as Vipassana. The term Vipassana translates into "insight or wisdom into reality" and that is precisely why it is also referred to as "insight meditation." This is one of the most ancient meditation practices that goes back to the 6th century BC.

Like other meditation techniques, there"s no right or ideal way to practice Vipassana or mindful meditation. A majority of practitioners start with mindful breathing or observing the breath in a judgment free manner. The practice then graduates to mindfully observing bodily sensations or thought patterns.

Qi Gong – Qi Gong is one of the oldest forms of Chinese meditation for boosting posture, respiration and relaxation. This meditation technique comprises using your breath to pass on energy throughout the body along with its core energy centers. There is a greater focus on movement and relaxing breathing methods. Qi Gong is excellent for reducing stress and stress induced conditions.

Transcendental – Transcendental meditation was founded by Maharishi Mahesh Yogi, and involves the use of a series of mantras for focusing and following one"s breath. The mantra differs according to a large number of factors, including the practitioner"s birth year or gender. Transcendental meditation is practiced by being in a seated position.

Movement Meditation – Movement meditation can be challenging for newbies, given the fact that it can be highly soothing and energizing all the same. The technique involves being seated and keeping your eyes closed, while concentrating on your breath, and trying out various flowing movements repetitively. Simply turn focus on the movement instead of a sound or thought or physical sensation. This can also be therapeutic for the body, and can boost circulation.

Reflective Meditation – Reflective meditation comprises reflecting upon a question, problem, topic or theme that requires contemplation or analysis. Practitioners gently draw the mind to a focused topic when it wanders. Conventionally, reflective meditation is used for gaining insight into the real meaning of perplexing concepts such as life, relationships, death, conscience and much more.

There are many professional or personal challenges we face in our day to day life, the conclusive insights to which lie in ancient philosophy and religious scriptures. Through contemplative and introspective meditation, we gain the needed wisdom and insights, which in turn leads to greater conviction. Practitioners will often be surprised at the breakthrough or innovative solutions they come up with through reflection or reflective meditation. This form of meditation is also valuable in understanding inner conflict issues that can come up as a result of a meditation practice.

Affirmation Meditation – Affirmation meditation is a technique that uses affirmations or positive thoughts as a way to firmly embed specific thoughts into the subconscious mind with the intention of manifesting these thoughts. The technique involves getting into a relaxed state, which makes the practitioner more suggestive. This helps the brain receive the message in more effective manner to influence your actions in the direction of the affirmation. Affirmations can involve physical health, focus, confidence, abundance, magnetism and much more.

Metta Meditation or Loving Kindness – This type of meditation comprises nurturing unconditional kindness and love for other living beings. Since kindness and empathy is the basis of Metta meditation, it is also referred to as compassion meditation. Research has suggested that a regular practice of Metta meditation leads to greater happiness, increased brain wave activity and balanced behavior.

Metta is love without any attachment and the objective is to boost a sense of harmony and goodwill for others. The practice starts with complete acceptance and unconditional love for oneself. The idea is to fully accept and love yourself before you can begin to love others unconditionally. This may not be one of the most popular meditation techniques but it can be equally effective when it comes to improving your mood and interpersonal relationships.

When practiced regularly, this form of mediation leads to absolute joy. This type of meditation is brilliant for practitioners suffering from negative thoughts, anger, aggression and depression. It is not possible to feel loving kindness and aggression at the same time. Metta meditation triggers your brain"s happiness centers.

Mantra Meditation – Mantra meditation is ideal for people who find serenity in repeating a positive mantra. It involves a single repetitive sound or bunch of sounds to empty the mind. By reciting a mantra or rhythmic song, the mind learns to release stress and develop keen focus. Mantras can either be sung loudly or repeated silently. A simple, effective yet powerful onomatopoeia is Ohm. The practice is ideal for beginners keen on maintaining a serious, disciplined and focused meditation practice.

Heart Centered Meditation – Heart centered is carried out to release negative energies, fears and grief. Its main objective is to heal the heart. The technique focuses on feeling a sense of connectedness with your heart and those of others. This meditation practice is especially useful for those suffering from a loss or grieving. It helps heal the heart and ease the pain of suffering.

Kundalini Meditation - The core philosophy of Kundalini meditation involves awakening the body"s dormant Kundalini energy (located at the end of your spine) through the power of meditation. Kunalini awakening is nothing but directing the energy up the spine, which is eventually believed to lead to an enlightened state. Kundalini meditation comprises a combination of breathing technique, hand placements (mudras) and chants (mantras). These tap into subconscious mind, and lead it to awaken, stimulate and energize the conscious mind. Open minded practitioners looking to explore their spirituality.

Chakra Meditation – Chakras are seven energy centers located in different regions of the body. Each of them is associated with a distinct sound, energy characteristic and color. Chakra meditations can be brilliantly combined with a yogic practice. The emphasis is on focusing on any physical or psychological aspect. Chakras meditations again use a combination of meditation techniques such as visualization, mudras and sound to heal a compelling emotional issue. Chakra meditations work well for those who are already practicing yoga, those looking to heal from an emotional or physical condition through energy and spiritually inclined practitioners.

Tonglen Meditation – Tonglen meditation is a Tibetian Buddhist discipline that is created for helping a practitioner connect with their suffering with the intention of helping them overcome it. The discipline"s premise is a total antithesis to the philosophy of the western world that subscribes to pleasure as a means of avoiding pain. Toglen trains you to manage suffering, pain and life's challenges. It helps you develop a sense of openness and acceptance for pain. It helps you release negativity, practice give and take, and nurture a sense of compassion through breathing, visualization techniques and powerful intention. Anyone dealing with stress, negativity, self doubt and difficult people can explore the benefits of Tonglen meditation.

CHAPTER 4

The 5-Minute Meditation

Duration – 5 minutes

Objective – To De-stress, Relax and Focus. These can also be used as warm ups for the more lengthier and intense meditation sessions described later in the book.

Setting – Begin by sitting in comfortable position. Use props such as cushions to seat yourself in a relaxed and comfortable posture. Practice in a serene and distraction free environment. Use aroma candles, incense or essential oils if required to create a soothing and energized setting.

Begin – Close your eyes.

Relax completely. Release all the tension from your body.

Spend a few minutes to gather yourself into the moment.

Let the breathing flow

Breathe in to the count of 1- 4 as your lungs expand

Breathe out to the count of 1-4 as your lungs contract

Allow each body muscle to relax as you breathe.

Let every ounce of stress fade away.

With each breathe out, exhale any leftover stress, worries and tension of the day

Allow yourself to relax completely

While breathing, imagine being on a lovely beach, while experiencing its warm, soothing and relaxing waves.

It is forming right at your toes with each deep breath you take.

The wave is slowly moving upwards.

It touches your feet first and slowly moves to your legs.

The wave then gradually touches your stomach and chest.

It moves to your arms, and finally above your head, relaxing and calming your body completely as your breathe. Your body is now completely free from any stress, tension or rigidity.

CHAPTER 5

10 Minute Guided Meditation Techniques

Meditation 1

Duration: 10 Minutes

Objective: To De-Stress, Relax, Concentrate and Sleep Better

We all know the mind can be exceedingly noisy. There"s so much chaos and clutter occupying our mind all the time. Most people believe that meditation isn"t suitable for them because they can"t halt their thoughts. However, this is the exact objective of meditation. Meditation is all about watching your thoughts come, evolve and go. It is about keenly tuning in to the thoughts. What we are doing is strengthening the attention muscle. Every time we recognize a thought and gently draw our focus back, we are building that vital attention/focus muscle. Think of meditation as a paper folding exercise. It takes focus, effort and diligence to get it right the first time around. However with time and practice, the act becomes seamless. Be gentle with yourself. Forcing yourself to meditate can be highly counterproductive. Treat the practice with some humor, kindness and curiosity. A popular meme doing rounds on the social media fittingly sums up the new age attitude towards mediation. It goes, "come on inner peace, I don't have all day." Don't try to force or induce peace into your being. Let it come gradually, naturally and soothingly.

Here's a 10 minute guided meditation you're absolutely going to love.

Find a comfortable seating position. Close your eyes when you are ready.

Pay close attention to your thoughts.

Notice the thoughts that pop into the head.

Are you thinking about what tasks need to done during the day or what just happened before you started meditating?

Simply notice your thoughts.

Take 3 cleansing breaths by inhaling through the nose and exhaling through your mouth.

Feel the breath completely and deep into your body.

Breathe into your chest and stomach.

Breathe into your ribs and back.

Each time the mind wanders, simply return to the breathing sensation and notice your breathing pattern. You mind will stray. It is natural. Bring it back gently into the physical sensations felt while breathing. Feel the wonderful air around you touching the tip of your nose. Notice how the air fills up your lungs.

Take the time to tune in to your environment

Closely notice the sounds surrounding you. What do you hear? The ventilation system hum? Sounds from the adjoining street? Birds chirping in your backyard? Gradually, start noticing the smallest sounds, including the sound of your breath.

Feel a sense of unison with the environment and yourself.

Be fully present. Catch yourself noticing thoughts.

Begin notice the things around you keenly. Start with the chair or seat on which your have positioned yourself.

Then, move on to the floor touching your feet.

Feel the air that touches your skin.

Start scanning your physical body.

Again, when you begin noticing thoughts occupying your mind, simply go back to the scanning process.

Start with your soles. Move up to the feet, calves, legs and thighs. Do not skip the joints. Do not simply think about the various body parts while scanning but actually feel them. Try and tune into the feeling each part induces. Notice is you experience any compelling emotions within the body. Do you feel any tension or soreness within the back, shoulders, joints and muscles? Do you notice any wandering thoughts? Simply pick up from where you left off.

Keep inhaling and repeat a mantra such as "breathe in", and exhale with "breathe out." Make it easy, natural and effortless. Each time your mind strays, get it back with the mantra, "breathe in" and "breathe out." Keep breathing in and out while repeating the mantra for a few seconds. Allow your mind to be free to expand its awareness. Think of this as watching a movie or listening to a song. How far can it really go? Its zoom out time.

Draw the awareness back to your body.

Keenly feel the chair you are sitting on.

Notice the air temperature against your skin.

Watch out sounds that you haven"t bothered about until now.

When you are done, open your eyes.

Notice where your thoughts are heading.

Are you excited about the task that"s coming up or are you able to experience a sense of stillness in the present?

Meditation 2

Duration: 10 Minutes

Objective: To De-Stress, Relax and Focus

Find a comfortable seating position and close your eyes once you are all set.

Let your mouth and jaw relax effortlessly. Find the perfect position. Do not clench it too tight or keep it wide open.

Begin with deep, soothing and relaxing breaths.

Breathe in through the nose and breathe out through the mouth.

Fill your lungs and stomach with the air through every breath.

Empty it through each exhalation.

Practice this multiple times.

Now get back to your natural breathing pattern.

Inhale and exhale through the nose. The breathing should be your normal breathing, easy and effortless. Let go of the urge to control the breath"s rhythm.

Continue breathing. Tune in to what is happening inside and around you.

Keep your ears open for different sounds.

Feel the chair you are sitting on.

Feel the skin of your feet touch the ground.

Just like the previous meditation, begin scanning your body. Start from your feet and move right up to the crown of the head. Take a few minutes to do this. Closely feel any sensations that originate. Draw awareness to different body parts as they you go on scanning upwards. Feel sensations without naming or labeling them as positive or negative.

Each time your mind wanders, gently carry it back to the sensations. Take some time out to reflect upon our mood. How do you feel today? Tune into any compelling emotions you are currently experiencing. Can you pinpoint the exact location where these emotions are housed? Is it your stomach or chest or head? Emotions can accumulate in several places within the body.

Concentrate on your breath now.

Start repeating the "breathe in" and "breathe out" mantra, while following your natural breathing pattern. Say "breathe in" each time you inhale and "breathe out" every time you exhale. Keep repeating the mantra, while keeping your attention firmly fixated on the tip of your nose.

Each time, you find your focus being challenged; simply get back to the breathing and mantra. Breathe in and breathe out. Recognize your drifting thoughts, and gently bring it back. Have you ever trained a puppy or witnessed one being trained? You have to guiding it back each time it wanders, with love, compassion and patience. Thoughts experienced during meditation are similar to training a puppy. They have to diverted to the point of focus with loving kindness and patience.

Breathe in and breathe out using the mantra.

Now breathe naturally without the mantra.

Now, set your mind free, expanding the realm of your attention as far as possible. Become completely aware of your senses. Feel your body weight. Tune in to the sounds engulfing your surroundings. Be aware of your breathing, thoughts and this voice directing you.

Can your mind simply take a step back from it all? Be aware of everything without actually being a part of it. Can you view things inside and around you objectively? Can you for a short-while act like a third person who is observing your life in a non-judgmental manner? Can you be the audience watching a movie on your life?

Now slowly come back to your body. Feel your breath. How does your body feel while coming in contact with the seat or chair? How does it feel when your feet touch the ground? Notice the sounds surrounding you. Enjoy an intense, deep and cleansing breath. Breathe in and out loudly. Tune in to the sound of your breath. Gradually open your eyes.

Meditation 3

The Smile and Stay Positive Meditation

Duration – 10 Minutes

Objective – To Stay Happy, Smiling and Positive.

Begin by finding a really comfortable and relaxing place to sit in. Wear comfortable clothes that keep you distraction free and at ease. Sit upright and be as comfortable as possible. Shut your eyes and draw attention to the breath. We begin by practicing deep breathing to calm your senses as your body and mind gradually relax. Inhale to the count of 1-4. Hold your breath at the last count. Breathe out at the count of 1-4.

Draw all the attention to the face. Is there any stress held in your jaw? Is the region behind your eyes, jaw and forehead feeling tensed? Let these regions relax and slow down. Let the cheeks relax completely. There"s no room for any stress or tension on your face. Your cheeks are gradually beginning to form a lovely smile.

Think of something really funny or amusing that happened in the past week. Think about your love for your near and dear ones. Think about all the numerous gifts you"ve been blessed with – a roof above your head, a hot cup of coffee to keep you warm in winters, warm and nutritious meals, the five senses with which you are able to experience the world around you.

You have a pair of footwear to keep your feet protected and clothes to keep you warm. There's so much to be grateful for in the world around you.

Focus on memories that make you happy. Think about a family reunion or a much awaited Thanksgiving/ Christmas meal. How does it feel to be surrounded by your loved ones? Focus on feelings, memories and instances that evoke a sense of happiness, joy and positivity in you.

If you feel tension accumulating within any part of the body, allow your smile to fix it gradually. Let the smile gently soften the region that is feeling stress and pain. Let the muscles soothe and relax. Stay here for a few seconds until you feel a complete sense of facial relaxation.

Next, move to the other body area that feels tensed, stressed and tight. Infuse a positive, inspiring and spirited smile into your sore muscles. As you infuse smile energy into them, feel the tiredness and soreness fading away. When you smile into stressed muscles, the tension is released. Allow the muscles to completely relax.

Draw awareness into the heart. Experience the heart feeling the warmth and calmness of your smile. Doesn"t your heart brim with happiness? Visualize a circle of love in the heart. As you smile into it, the circle grows. It is now full of pure love energy. The heart is throbbing with this pure, positive and inspiring love energy. The circle grows bigger with every smile you put into it. The love energy is emitting a sparkling pink light. The light represents love and healing. Few things in life are as healing as unconditional love originating from a pure heart. Feel the love and healing coming from your heart. Focus on how your heart feels. Keep this focus for a few seconds. Focus only on the love growing in your heart"s energy circle.

While focusing on the heart, here are some positive affirmations that you can repeat now and throughout the day to brighten up your spirit.

"I am happy, positive and relaxed irrespective of the circumstances."

"The power to remain happy, positive and unaffected lies within me."

"I find it increasingly simple to smile, stay positive and spread happiness."

"I alone am responsible for my well-being and happiness."

"The key to my happiness is in my hands alone."

"Happiness shines easily on me."

"When I am happy, smiling and positive, the whole world is happy with me."

Now, slowly draw awareness to the face again. How do you feel now? Is there a greater feeling of happiness, positivity and lightness? Now, when the session is over, it"ll be simpler for you to smile and stay more positive all through the day. It is time to awaken from the meditative state. Slowly, start brining your body and mind into a state of awareness. When you feel sufficiently ready, gradually start opening your eyes. You are now in a waking consciousness state. Get up and be prepared to spread your joy, happiness, smile, love and positivity all around you.

CHAPTER 6

The Fifteen Minute Anxiety Killing And Confidence Building Guided Meditation

Meditation 1

Duration: 15 minutes

Objective: To overcome anxiety, build confidence and ensure complete relaxation.

The meditation that we are just about to guide you is great for relaxation, combating anxiety and building self-esteem. This one"s great for helping you feel more relaxed, guiding you towards fading your anxieties and helping you clear the mind. Lastly, it helps you find a soothing serenity within the self, where you feel complete safety and calmness.

Make yourself completely comfortable. Sit down in a place that is calm, positively energized and distraction free. You want a place where your worries, stress and problems can melt away.

Let's begin all you rockstar practitioners.

Shut your eyes, and breathe deeply. Release the breath.

Try and blank out your thoughts. Keep it free from worries. Simply experience stillness and silence. You have a powerful soul. It is stronger than you think. It can guide your body into feeling relaxed and rejuvenated. It has the capacity to heal, nurture, soothe, calm and replenish your spirit. It has the power to mend your broken heart, spirit and confidence. It gives you joy, confidence, glory, happiness and positivity.

Focus on your breath. Notice the oxygen making its way into the nose gradually. Breathe out slowly. When you exhale, concentrate on the pain that's haunting you. It can be physical or psychological. Know that you are not alone in your suffering. No harm can come upon you. This is the ideal place to be where your stress, concerns, anxiety and self doubt doesn't have footholes.

Imagine being on your favorite beach in the world. Feel the soft, flowy and golden sand touching your feet. Feel the gentle, balmy and summery breeze caressing your hair and face. Imagine the warmth of the morning sunshine against your skin. Visualize the images appearing before you. Imagine the ocean"s vastness and infinity. Picture waves crashing against the coast. Immerse into the relaxing and calming sound of the waves. Let it completely fill your mind and relax the body. Feel a growing sense of relaxation beginning to take over your head, neck, shoulders, arms, hands and back. The relaxation is absolutely pure, soothing and intense.

Feel the relaxation slowly enveloping your legs, and then gradually moving to the feet. Your eyes are still shut. Breathe normally. Fill your mind with positivity, gentleness and light. Become aware of your greatness. There is an intensely sparkling light inside your mind, like no one else. Think about the illuminating and incandescent aura you carry around you. There"s no one in the Universe like you. Know that you are capable of achieving much more than you believe with your uniqueness. There is a constant light within you that is leading you towards the greatness you deserve.

Relax now. Get yourself ready to go back to your regular state, filled with a renewed sense of light, positivity and magnificence. Slowly, start gaining awareness of your surroundings. Be prepared to live in peace and harmony not just with yourself but also with your surroundings. Stay still for some time. Enjoy the blissfulness of the place where you are completely and positively yourself.

Take a few deep breaths. Relax. Smile confidently. You are now completely ready to take on the world with your newfound positivity and self-assured smile. The world is waiting to embrace your greatness with open arms. Relax. Slowly open your eyes.

Meditation 2

Loving: Kindness Meditation

Duration: 15 Minutes

This particular exercise draws from the guided meditation put together by researcher Emma Seppala, Director of Science at the

Stanford University''s Center for Compassion and Altruism Research and Education and the author of The Happiness Track.

Close your eyes slowly. Be seated in comfortable position with your feet placed on the floor and the spine held upright. Relax the entire body. Keep your eyes shut during the entire visualization exercise for more reflective and inward awareness. Do not strain yourself or force yourself to concentrate. Simply relax and follow simple instructions. Take a deep breath in and exhale.

Monitor your breathing pattern as the chest gradually rises. Keep your eyes shut. Think of an individual who is very close to your heart. That person is standing to your right. The person loves you a lot. It could be someone you knew in the past or a person who occupies an important space in your present. The person is standing next to you now, transferring all the love, positivity, assurance and warmth your way from the person. The person wishes you safety, health, happiness, wellness and kindness. Feel the pure love and warmth coming your way.

Visualize another person standing on your left. This is a person who cherishes and loves you deeply. He/she is sending you plenty of wishes for your happiness, wellness and health. Feel a sense of positivity, kindness, warmth and compassion coming your way from this wonderful person.

Now, picture yourself being encircled by all the people you've loved dearly in your life and all those who love you or have loved you in the past. Imagine being surrounded by family, friends, loved ones and well-wishers. They are sending you positive wishes and love from everywhere. Your spirit is overflowing with love, positivity, warmth and happiness.

Breathe in slowly. Now breathe out. Relax. Draw your focus back on the individual to your right. Start sending love to the person and experience him/her sending it back to you. You and the person are alike. This individual also seeks happiness like you. Send all the love, warmth, positivity and good wishes to this person.

Draw your awareness back to the person on your left. Start sending love to him/her. Send all the warmth and positivity you can. You and the person are pretty similar to each other. This individual also wishes for happiness, just like you. Send all the love, warmth, positivity and good wishes to this person.

Think of a neutral acquaintance. Someone you haven"t had a chance to know well enough, and who you do not have strong feelings of love or hate for. The only common aspect is that both you and this person desire to lead a good life. Send well-being wishes to this person.

Slowly, expand your awareness and visualize the entire planet. The little globe that holds the entire world is now held in the realm of your mind"s eye. Think of it as a small ball. Send encouraging and positive wishes to every living being on planet earth. They are all like you. Just like you, they wish to be experiences complete happiness.

Take a deep and intense breath. Breathe out. Take another deep breath and let go. Simply notice how your mind feels after the session. Open your eyes slowly once you"re ready.

Meditation 3

Anger and Pain Releasing Meditation

Duration: 15 Minutes

Objective: To release anger and pain held within us.

You many have experienced trauma, violence or mental abuse in your childhood, which may have created a huge reservoir of anger, pain, guilt and resentment within you. You aren"t alone. There are millions of people who have suffered abuse in their childhood, which has had a direct bearing on their thoughts, emotions and actions. This meditation session will help you gradually release pent up anger, and be in a peaceful space. If you feel overwhelmed or overcome by emotions at any stage, simply pause. Practice deep breathing and get back to the session when you feel more mentally ready

for it. You can leave it for a better time if it gets tough. Just do not force yourself to continue when you feel uncomfortable during the meditation process.

Start by taking a few deep and intense breaths. Be completely aware of your breath and you breathe in and out. Inhale slowly. Exhale. Perform this deep breathing exercise for some time till you feel relaxed and more centered. When you inhale, imagine breathing in an incandescent white light into your body. When you breathe out, visualize releasing all the pent up tension, guilt and anger from your body.

Now imagine catching the film of your life in a large and comfortable cinema theatre. The lights have been slowly dimmed. The screen has suddenly lit up to play the movie. Now, it comes alive with a past memory. This is the memory of the thing that caused you intense pain, hurt and anger. Someone from your childhood brought in unpleasant memories of hurt and anger. Now this painful memory is slowly being played on the screen.

See everything you can and try to stay detached from it. View it as an objective audience with no room for attachment or emotions, the way movie critics do when they review films. Look around and see if someone else is present in the theatre. This is the same person from your past who has scarred you. The person is also watching the memory movie play out in front of their eyes. They are getting slightly uncomfortable, yet cannot escape their past actions.

This person is now getting an account of the pain, hurt and suffering experienced by you as the movie unfolds. The individual is now feeling sad and shedding tears. He/she slowly approaches you and begs your forgiveness. You are in a sort of a complex emotional state yourself, still processing the pain and trauma of the hurtful memory.

Understand that now you are in a completely protected and comfortable space. You are feeling more self-assured, peaceful and empowered. You are in a space where this person slowly ceases to affect you. You are now involved in a conversation with the person who has hurt you. You gently tell them that the past is gone, and that you have forgiven them. You tell them that the hurt they caused you due to their past actions is now a thing of the past that has no relevance to your present or future.

The theatre gradually begins to be filled with a magical violet light. The entire room is engulfed in the magnificence of this radiant violet light. It is as if some magical force has come into being suddenly to take away all your hurt, trauma and pain. Your pain, stress and hurt have evaporated into this shinning violet light. Tears flow from your eyes, but you realize that you are healing at a deeper level. When you inhale, the heart gradually opens. There is deep love, forgiveness and light filling your heart. The love has completely taken over the heart in a surreal, almost magical healing process.

You have now walked ahead and reached over to the person who caused you pain. This person is now held in an embrace by you. Your heart is open now. The multiple layers of anger, suffering, pain and discomfort are evaporating. There is a release and healing

process taking place at a deep level. There is now no guilt, anger, regret, remorse or pain. The feelings may come back as you try to release them. Acknowledge them. Stay with them for as long as it takes to heal you until the negative feelings are completely released. Your soul knows exactly how to heal itself. The challenge here lies in silencing the mind. Bring and soul and mind in unison until you feel a sense of calmness and peace.

Now, the violet light is gradually transforming into a beautiful green light. The anger has transformed into magical healing. The green light has completely surrounded you, healing every layer of your physical and metal self. The green light fades slowly. The screen has now gone blank. The lights are gradually turned on. The green light is passing through every heart cell, infusing it with forgiveness and healing. No region of your heart remains untouched by the magnificence of the green, healing light. You are awash with a profound feeling of peace, forgiveness and love. There is no absolutely no room for pain, guilt, hurt and regret.

You feel complete and immune to pain now. Results may vary from person to person. While some may move over their past quickly, others may require a few sessions to release pent up negative emotions. This can be practiced multiple times until you all your anger, guilt, pain and trauma has evaporated. Every ounce of anger should melt from your physical, mental and spiritual self before you stop this session.

Get ready to move your awareness back into the waking consciousness. Draw awareness to your body by breathing slowly and gently. Open your eyes slowly. You are now ready to take on the world with a renewed sense of forgiveness.

CHAPTER 7

The Twenty Minute Body Scan

Duration: 20 minutes

Objective: To experience a sense of calmness and gratitude.

The meditation is fundamentally important for killing fear, denial and awkwardness associated with developing familiarity with your body. It helps develop a deep sense of awareness, understanding and unconditional love for the body, simply for nourishing you and keeping you alive. Practitioners learn to explore the body"s fragility, tendency for injury and fragility. They learn to rise above pain and illness. You learn to cope with the eventuality of aging. Above all – there is a greater acceptance for what it is. There is a greater feeling of disenchantment yet complete compassion and peace with the physical body. There is a reduced tendency to become experience shock, distress or grief at getting injured, feeling hungry, growing old or becoming ill. By employing the body as study mechanism, practitioners learn to cope with the body"s warning signals.

To set the record straight, beginners may not be able to instantly slip into a daily 15-minute meditation session. People fail to establish a 15 minute and half hour routine right at the onset of their practice, only to express disappointment for the practice altogether. "Oh! It didn"t work for me." Meditation is not different from mastering any discipline. It involves taking baby steps, mastering one small goal at the time before you leap to bigger ones. Take baby steps by meditating for 5 minutes a day to begin with. Gradually increase the duration to 10-15 minutes daily.

Be consistent and disciplined about the practice. Try and reserve a fixed hour for your meditation practice each day. This will bring about a greater sense of consistency and routine to it. Once you keep practicing it, it will become an enjoyable habit, a happy addiction that"s tough to discard. Okay, even if you don"t enjoy it like as much as a deep dish pizza, you"ll still no longer feel a sense of anticipation, compulsion or dread about going through the practice.

Pro Tip – if you aren"t following a guided audio or video meditation and are always worried sick about exceeding your meditation duration, set a timer on your phone. This way you do not have to keep wondering how the number of minutes still left to practice. Find a serene, low-lit place. Some folks may prefer a bright or naturally-lit space. It all depends on what soothes your senses, while elevating your spirit all the same.

To do a body scan meditation, be aware of various body parts such as arms, legs and torso. Mentally note the exact location of each of these bodily components. Start to divide them further into more intricate details. For instance, the arm can become the wrist, fingers, shoulder, elbow, palm and so on. Spend time on gaining awareness of
every part, including the sensations that are felt on it. Body awareness is not just about

gaining awareness but being completely aware of how each component feels, where exactly it is housed and what its true purpose is.

There are several other benefits of a body scan meditation.

Several practitioners have found this technique to work wonderfully for pain management, boosted immunity, focused relaxation and greater physical responsiveness. You allow a compassionate, soothing and healing energy to pass into your being. There is a greater need to allow the body part to relax, repair and heal, which reduces stress and worry related issues.

What you are basically doing is a mental body CT scan. Have you ever seen CT scans? You can view your muscles, bones and internal organs. This is exactly what your mind is going to do in a body scan meditation. You may end up experiencing sensations or being completely aware of a particular body part.

Begin – Sit on a chair with overlapped hands. Sitting on the ground can be uncomfortable for many. Keep your back straight and head held up.

Shut your eyes slowly. Don"t do it all mechanically. Take time to slip into the position and gradually start closing your eyes.

Gently, start checking in with the body. Notice how your toes feel. Move on to other parts of the body, including the legs, belly, torso and head.

How do your legs feel? Are they still or is there some movement in them? What sensations are you currently experiencing in your legs? Keep your focus on your legs and blank out other body parts. How does the skin on your leg feel? Do you feel a potent force in your legs that carries your entire body? How do the toes that are touching the ground feel. What sensations do you experience in your feet? Tune in very closely to the physical sensations felt in your toes, feet and legs.

Bring complete awareness to your breathing. Breathe in and breathe out. Notice touching the floor and feeling a sense of touch when your feet make contact with the floor or a chair. Take time to experience and explore each section of your body. How does your body feel when you breathe in let in a gush of air into it? Experience the feeling closely. What sensation does the body feel when exhale a gush of air from the body.

Move to any region of your choice. Where exactly is it located in the body? What is its purpose within the cycle of your bodily functions? How did it originate? What does it need to sustain? Examine the experiences of the mind. How does the mind complement the body? For instance, when the mind experiences stress, the heart rate changes and muscles feel tense. Practice breathing in and out intentionally. You may do a complete body scan starting from the head and going right up to the feet. Sensations can also be explored or investigated randomly.

Your experiences can include a tingling sensation, temperature, pressure or just about anything that is noticed. Sometimes, you may not feel anything at all. Things may just be neutral. That is alright too. Notice these neutral feelings nevertheless. There"s no good and bad, no wrong or right. Simply tune in to the present without judgment. It"ll change the way you start perceiving things. Keep your mind open, curious and compassionate to whatever sensations you are exploring.

Now, release focus from whichever region, you were concentrating on and move to explore another part.

At some point you may start thinking about the last Game of Thrones you watched, and find your focus wandering. Wonderful! It simply means that you are noticing your mind straying. You'll know quickly into the practice that the mind cannot help wandering. However, over a period of time, it will be trained to be still for a longer duration. The idea is to gently and compassionately train it and not force it. Draw attention to exploring your bodily sensations. Neuroscience has pointed to the fact that simply noticing our wandering attention and then bringing it back gradually and gently to our object/thought/area of focus creates new brain pathways.

Try and think about your personal experiences of the mindbody interaction. How does the body actually feel when there is an underlying fear, stress, uneasiness and tension? When the mind is calm, soothing and relaxed, how exactly does your body feel? When the mind is completely relaxed, doesn't the body feel exceedingly relaxed as well?

Is there any sense of attachment or wish that occurs in connection with a body part? What feelings are experienced by the mind when you spot something really beautiful and positive?

When you graduate to the head, imagine a soothing white room. Focus on your mentally created room. There will some buzzing in your mind. Focus on it too. Sometimes, you will invariably find yourself concentrating on nothing, which is wonderful too. Your mind will be hijacked with thoughts about what"s cooking for supper or a string urge to scratch your feet. These are natural. Such moments will occur throughout your meditation practice, however long you"ve been practicing for. Simply let go of the distracting thought with patience, compassion and gentleness. Bring your focus back on those "nothingness" thoughts or the white room.

When you finish the exploratory body sensations scan, take a few minutes for expanding your realm of attention. Feel your body breathing without any restrictions. Slowly open your eyes.

Meditation is not about eliminating or discarding distracting thoughts. It is accepting that the mind wanders, as long as you can recognize when it happens and get yourself back to your focus. Now, open your eyes slowly and get back to the real world. Boost your capacity to draw complete attention on real time feelings and sensations involving nothing but the present.

Train the mind slowly to accept both the pleasant and not so pleasant sensations. Learn to notice simply by being there and noticing what's going on in the body rather than feeling the urge to fix everything that causes discomfort.

Don't you experience a renewed sense of familiarity, acceptance and understanding with your physical faculties? Isn't there a greater sense of gratitude for the gifts you've been blessed with? Don't you feel blessed for the physical, mental and spiritual gifts you've been endowed with?

CHAPTER 8

The 25 Minute Blissful Mind Meditation

Duration: 25 Minutes

Objective – Attaining a blissful and relaxed state of being.

Ensure that you are wearing loose and comfortable clothing. Let your hands lie loosely on the lap.

Let"s begin.

Shut your eyes. Relax completely.

With shut eyes, start connecting with the world inside you. Be aware of your internal feelings and thoughts. Slowly, blank out the external world from your realm of awareness. Take a few minutes to give yourself the freedom to enjoy a soothing and relaxing experience. For a few minutes, you are completely liberated from all responsibilities. Discard thoughts of tasks that are waiting to be completed. If you catch your mind straying during the session, gently draw the awareness back to the sound that is guiding you towards complete relaxation, tranquility and stillness.

You are always in control. If you desire to stop the session, just open your eyes. Take a slow extended breath. Release your breath. Feel yourself relaxing completely.

Take an extended, deep and slow breath again. Release it.

Take another deep and intense breath. Exhale.

Simply notice the calmness in the breath. Become aware of a relaxed feeling that is beginning to engulf your entire body.

Continue breathing slowly, deeply, compassionately and gently.

Notice your thoughts becoming lighter. They are now gradually floating in the air. They are drifting in the air, slowly moving up into the universe. The thoughts are becoming lighter and lighter and making their way further up into the air. The thoughts have now drifted far away, yet are accessible when you want them to be. They haven"t left your conscious state permanently. The thoughts are only helping you attain a state of gentle bliss and relaxation.

Experience a profound spaciousness developing inside you. The space inside you is completely empty now.

Relax completely.

Let the gentle movement of the breath direct you into a completely relaxed state.

Breathe in and out. Go deeper into your being.

Again in and out. Let your mind gradually slow down.

Breathe in and out.

You are in a completely relaxed state now. It is now time to begin a guided journey into a place of tranquility and bliss.

Allow visuals to be created in your naturally.

If mental visuals are hard to come by, just enjoy a sensory experience of your dream surroundings than viewing them in the mind"s eye.

Release all expectations. Allow yourself to witness the guide journey in a natural and seamless manner.

Start imagining that you are on a lush and lovely grassy field.

Feel the sun"s warmth caressing your body and face.

The breeze is slowly making its way towards you.

Feel the soft, dew-drops filled grass under your naked feet. The moisture is gently kissing the tips of your toes.

Witness the haunting sounds of nature surrounding you.

Feel the hustling of the lush green tree"s soothing branches.

There"s a waterfall in the background, which is making a haunting and soothing gushing sound as it elegantly cascades. The sound of flowing water instills a sense of energy and calmness in your spirit. You feel a deep sense of harmony with nature. Nature is soothing you and energizing you all the same with its magnificence.

Become aware of a bird"s pleasant song slowly originating in the background. It gets louder with every breath you take.

Feel the sound of the wind blowing through your hair. It is touching your face and hair with its natural magnificence. It is moving from your face and hair to your shoulders, chest and belly. It gradually makes its way to your legs, feet and toes. The hustling wind symbolizes an indomitable spirit that tests your strength and offers you respite from the heat all the same.

You are home in the idyllic destination. A safe haven. This is the place you belong to. This is your space. This is where your mind, body and spirit experience and unmatched sense of unison. You are free from stress, anxiety and nervousness here. There is no time to worry. You are filled with extreme positivity and elation.

You have a lot of time at hand. There is no rush to head anywhere or get anything done. This time is yours alone.

There is a deep feeling of safety and happiness.

There is not stress or anxiety touching you here. You are only living in a state of pure, undisturbed and unaffected bliss.

Take time out to appreciate the surroundings you live in.

Become aware of a big tree growing in the vicinity.

There are lots of birds happily chirping on the branches of this tree.

Begin walking towards the tree. Feel relaxed yet energized with every step you take towards the tree. Feel yourself going closer to the tree with each deep breath. You are now standing facing the magnificent, gigantic and marvelous creation of nature. Nature"s wonders never cease to amaze your spirit. You experience an incomparable feeling of communion with nature.

Take time to become completely aware of each moment and fully experience every step. Be aware of everything you do without judging it. If distracting thoughts make their way into the mind, be aware of them and gently put them aside to focus on the powerful imagery.

Feel yourself getting into a deep state of relaxation. You are slowly but surely reaching a state of blissful relaxation.

Stand beneath the tree. Feel its sturdy branches and huge leaves stand above your head. Experience a strong feeling of protection under its glorious shelter. Nature is a brilliant healer and protector. It alleviates our woes to help us slip into a state of positivity, elation and hopefulness. Experience your stress melting away slowly as you become one with nature.

The tree is completely enveloped with delicious and juicy fruits of various colors, shapes and sizes. This is isn"t an ordinary tree. Its fruits have extraordinary powers. Imagine its sweet, ripe and delicious fruits falling all around you.

Reach out and enjoy a fruit piece. Examine the fruit closely for some time. What is the color of the fruits? What is its weight, size and texture?

Take a big bite now. Experience the fruit filling up your mouth.

As the fruit enters your throat and stomach, an amazing thing happens.

A feeling of deep happiness starts to grow deep within you.

The sensation originates in the stomach and travels all the way to the heart, lungs and chest.

Release thinking. Focus on nothing else but the feeling. Cherish this sensation of well-being and gentle love. Feel your spirit light up.

Take another fruit bite. Savor its sweet, juicy and delicious taste.

The amazing feeling has grown even more intense now.

Feel yourself glowing with a strong sensation of happiness, well-being and love.

Take another bite of the wonder fruit. The big can be as big as you want. Eat as much as you can. Relish its sweet spirit.

Relax completely and let yourself be overcome with a delightful feeling. Do not force yourself to do it. Simply let it take over your spirit effortlessly. Let it grow as much as you wish it to. Let it cover your entire body. Let every cell within your body experience this feeling of delightfulness and bliss.

Now, visualize yourself on an idyllic beach. It is a warm, bright and sunny day. The weather isn"t too hot. There is a pleasant and light breeze. You are gradually feeling the warmth of the sun infusing energy into your skin. Hear the refreshing and gentle waves licking the sand. Enjoy your communion with nature. You are experiencing a complete sense of oneness with nature.

There is no one else on the lovely beach. Yet, you feel a complete sense of safety. There is no danger lurking around anywhere. You are in an absolutely safe, secure and private space. You remove your footwear and place them on the flowy, balmy and golden sand. Experience how the tiny sand particles feel against your feet. Imagine walking on the warm, invigorating and energy infusing sand. There is a low sound of seagulls prancing above the water. The sound is faint yet audible. It adds a deep sense of tranquility to the setting.

You are now beginning to walk towards the pristine water. Walk adjacent the shore, where the sand, rocks and water meet. The sand feels soft, calm and cool. There is a pleasant breeze blowing in the air. The air is pure, fresh and rejuvenating. Slowly, let the

tension in your body evaporate as you walk in the sand. With every step you take, the tension is decreasing. All your stress, worries and tensions are slowly fading away. There"s no room for anxiety here. It is all peace, calm and relaxation.

Take a deep breath and breathe out slowly. Take another intense breath and breathe out gradually and gently. Experience the life force elements of nature refilling your senses

with calmness and energy. Visualize any region in your body that feels aches, tensions and pains. Now imagine this stress slowly passing away and being released from your body. As water flows to the shore, it washes away all your tiredness, stress and worries. It all flows away along with the water. You are now in an absolute state of serenity and idyllic peace on the beach.

Now, a strong wave comes gushing to the shore. You bend down slightly and spot a bottle neat your foot. Instinctively, you reach out to pick it up. The bottle is now in your hands. It is cork sealed with a message note held within it. You pull open the cork, and expectantly reach out for the paper held inside the bottle. Experience gradually unfolding the paper and reading everything that"s written in there.

"For whoever reads these words, understand that this message is to reach out to you and let you know how special your actually are. You are unique and eternally loved. I have picked you to receive love, and pass it around to other people and planet earth. Help them heal. Never for a second doubt about how special you are or your power to change the world." – The Universe.

On the reading the words, you are elated beyond measure. There is a deep sense of being able to touch other lives, which is why you want several others to discover this message in a bottle. You neatly fold the piece of paper and place it in the bottle. The bottle is resealed. Now, you throw it back to where it came from so someone else can find it. The bottle has made its way into the ocean to inspire and touch some more lives along the way. The positivity chain has been carried forward. The good that was sent to you from the Universe and has been sent back to the Universe.

The Universe has just conveyed to you that you are special and loved. Now, slowly visualize an angel approaching towards you. The angel is carrying a huge box that is filled with jigsaw puzzle pieces. You are now asked to pick pieces of your choice in whichever color, shape and image you like right there on the beach. The pieces are all arranged on the sand. The angel slowly whispers into your ear that you are just about to put together a puzzle of your existence. It says this and slowly walks away from, fading into the horizon.

You now have the freedom to select any images you like and complete the puzzle of your life. Pick words, shapes, symbols and colors that bear a special significance in your life. Select images that are especially meaningful for you. Put the pieces together seamlessly as you create the ideal life picture. Take a few minutes to visualize the puzzle you've created. How has this puzzle turned out? Reflect on your choices by spending a few reflective and peaceful moments.

It is slowly time to move out of the meditation. Start bringing your body into a state of awareness. Feel the glowing force take over your entire body. Start with the toes, move up the feet, ankles, legs, thighs, stomach, chest, shoulders, neck, face and head. The glow has now taken over your entire body. You are completely relaxed and in a state of bliss now. Slowly open your eyes. Take a few seconds to gather yourself and gain awareness of the waking consciousness. Get ready for a joyful and blissful day ahead or a calm, relaxed night ahead.

CHAPTER 9

The 30 -Minute Meditation

Duration – 30 Minutes

Objective – Complete Relaxation of the Body, Mind and Spirit.

Sit in a comfortable posture. Relax completely to release any stress from your muscles. Sit upright and avoid slumping. The ideal would be a clam yet alert state. Maintain your regular attentive posture to prevent yourself from falling asleep. You can also simply lay down and meditate. Do what works best for you.

Let us begin the meditation session now.

Start by taking many deep breaths. Keep the focus on your stomach, and continue breathing. Let the mind relax. Forget your worries. Remember, you are now in a safe haven where nothing can stress you. Take deep, slow and intense breaths. Imagine air entering your belly.

We will now utilize the power of color energy to eliminate stress from the body. Visualize a serene green light circle taking shape right above your head. The energy circulates in waves and drips on you. It is everywhere now. The green waves are dripping all around you. They have encircled you. The light energy is moving gradually, changing into cocoons encircling the body. The green light energy is forming a protective and healing circle around you for as long as you are meditating. It starts from the head and goes right down to the feet.

Every time you inhale from the nose, you are drawing in green energy from the cocoon. Pull the green energy into the body, down to your belly. Feel the energy spreading through the body and eliminating stress as you breathe out. Imagine the energy spreading internally as you breathe. It is soothing and relaxing. The green energy circulates within the body. It pushes out negative energy with each breath out.

Visualize the breath and the energy flowing within. Hear the energy in motion as it makes sounds along with the tune of your breath.

The energy soothes and relaxes your muscles. As green energy moves in the body, all the negative energy is pushed out with every breath out.

Imagine this energy gradually moving to your head, then slowly taking over the lungs and moving outwards. The energy is soothing the muscles it passes through. You can lead this powerful energy wherever you desire. You are simply borrowing from the vast reserves of energy that are encircling you and moving all around you.

Every time you borrow this energy within the body, you end up experiencing a greater feeling of relaxation and control. Feel this powerful energy on your face. Feel it

revitalizing and rejuvenating the muscles on the face. It is now loosening, soothing and relaxing all your muscles. Relax the forehead. Shut your eyes. Let the energy slowly move into your cheeks and finally take over the jaw. Feel all your muscle tension and stress melting away. Now exhale completely. Feel the facial muscle tension being released.

The energy is now completely moving through your breath, down to the neck. It circulates in a swirly pattern, encircling the complete neck region. The energy is doing nothing but easing your neck muscles, while letting you breathe more easily. The tightened muscles have been opened. They are now completely relaxed. Exhale to feel stress within the neck region melt away. It is slowly leaving your body.

Inhale deeply. Feel the energy taking over your shoulder and chest muscles now. The energy touches the muscles and completely de-stresses them. Your shoulders droop slightly and the chest stays still while you breathe deeply. Breathe gently by breathing in and out the belly. Keep the shoulders and chest completely relaxed now. Experience the energy taking over the chest and shoulder region, and releasing any pent up tension. Fully relax your muscles. Breathe out and witness all your tensions fade away while breathing.

As you breathe in, witness the energy moving down to your arms. The energy takes over your arms, right down to every finger. The energy flows down your biceps and triceps, letting the muscles feel rejuvenated and relaxed. All the injuries and pain you"ve accumulated in the region through daily athletic or desk job activities are dwindling away. The energy is releasing pain and substituting it with a strong feeling of renewal.

Gradually relax your wrists. Take each finger at a time. Experience each finger being filled with a healing energy. As you exhale, the energy is passing through your arms, taking the pent up negative energy. It leaves your arms that toil hard throughout the day, feeling lighter, renewed and more stressfree.

Relax the stomach that has been letting this energy into the body. Let the flow of your breathe relax it and infuse it with even more energy. The muscles in motion are now completely relaxed, making the way for your internal organs to receive a soothing massage, which takes the relaxation process even further.

On the next breath, feel the energy flowing deeper into the stomach and taking over the entire pelvic region. The energy fills your hips and gently relaxes all muscles and organs held within the pelvic region. This supreme energy draws the region into a state of harmony. It releases pent up sexual tension. When you breathe out, the stress in your pelvic area and hips is released from the body, leaving a warm and refreshed feeling.

Now, you will suck the energy deep into your legs to fill up your leg muscles. Think about the legs that hold the weight of your body. They help you move around through

the day. Can you imagine the build-up of stress and tension? It will all be released soon. Breathe deeply. Every breathe fills your legs with energy, starting with the thighs, and gradually move downwards. As the energy passes through your legs, allow the muscles to ease up. Your thighs are now completely limp with zero stress residing in there.

The energy is gradually moving through your knees, soothing any pain and injuries with a replenished healing sensation. The energy is dripping down your calf muscles. It is flowing to your shins. The energy brings all your tension and stress to the ground. All the stress is evaporating through your feet. Feel the energy slowly moving up the ankle now. The energy begins to take over your feet. Experience the muscles within your feet relax completely. The energy spills into every toe and slowly moves towards the feel pads. Feel it relaxing the heels. The energy is actively working towards releasing all the pain and tension housed in the region by walking.

When you breathe out, green energy is released through the feet, getting back to its original cocoon. All your body tension, stress and pain evaporate with this green energy. The body is now encircled by a rejuvenated circle of energizing, calming and healing energy. With every breath you take, your body is filled with a deep sense of healing and calmness. Continue to heal, soothe your senses and relax as we continue.

We will continue the meditation by slipping into a deeper state of relaxation and bliss. As you enter a deeper meditation state, you are absolutely in control of your being and the energy that transverses through your being. Even from inside, the energy remains with you, offering you a more positive, healing and rejuvenating protection.

Now that you are completely relaxed, forget about the body. Allow the consciousness to be directed solely on your inner world. Move inwards. Allow the imagery to uncover from within your inner self. Visualize yourself being protected by the energy cocoon. You are now safely seeing everything unfolding before you in the powerful mind"s eye.

A circular white halo of energy suddenly starts to take shape below you. This is only but a means of taking you into a more intense state of consciousness. It will transport you into a universe of absolute peace. Imagine an elevator gradually lifting you into a deeper state of consciousness. You have complete control of the elevator as you breathe.

When you breathe in, the white energy ring sparkles and takes life, getting ready to take you into deeper mental levels. While breathing out, the elevator slowly lowers down. Experience the floor under you taking slow yet firm motions. There"s absolutely no danger. You are in a protected and secure personal zone that has been created only by you. Tune into the soothing humming sound of the elevator. Now you see the numerical 1 just above the head.

Under the numerical 1 is the word Relax, glowing in a bright blue neon shade.

Breathe in deep into the belly. Let the green energy completely soak your body. Move slightly lower mentally. Stay aware, calm and alert nevertheless. When you breathe out, you move through number 2 just over the head. Again, the word Relax sparkles just below number 2 is bright neon blue. Once you see the incandescent word, you feel a

deeper sense of relaxation and comfort. The glowing light keeps humming as one moves deeper. You are heading to a solid, powerful and secure place. Inhale now. Keep increasing the green energy housed within you. Mentally, move lower now. Breathe out. Release negative energy. Witness the numerical 3, along with Relax. Relax is getting larger and more prominent with each subsequent level.

Let the subsequent inhalation take you lower. You are now into a state that is deeper than you"ve experienced in the session. The green energy is now more intense than you"ve ever witnessed. It is held with the protective circle. It can be found flowing and moving around freely, while still being with you. The energy is gradually growing within you as you take slow, deep breaths. All the negative energy is slowly being pushed out. You exhale and view number 4 just above the head. There is the Relax word again, becoming even more defined and larger than before.

You are now located halfway there. All your negative energy has been kept behind. As you breathe in and move deeper, the energy increases within you. You are completely soaked with this profound, intense, powerful and positive energy. All the negative energy has been released and left behind at the previous level.

Breathing out completely, you go through level 5, and spot Relax just above it. It is now conspicuous and clearly visible in the mind"s eye. There"s no difficulty in viewing it. Even if you cannot spot the word, feel its vibrations. Hear it being played out several times in the head. Hear the word Relax gaining strength and guiding you every step of the way.

Take a few deep breaths. You are heading into a more intense state of relaxation. All the accumulated negativity has been abandoned. Focus on letting it all go. Release all your tensions, stress and worries. Nothing will bother you now. You are in a safe, stress-free and serene space. Nothing will affect you here. Any sounds you catch now will make the process of slipping into your space even deeper. The noises are distant. Nothing can distract your or take away from your concentration.

Take a long, deep breath into your belly. Extend the stomach outwards. The chest feels more relaxed. The air passes deeper into the lungs effortlessly. Take a deep breath now. Move lower. Breathe out deeply. You now see spot number 6 and feel the term Relax on your body. It has enveloped your entire body. It can be spotted and heard, becoming more and more intense, while helping you.

Take a pleasant and intense breath. Gradually, move into a deeper state. When you breathe out, number 7 is shinning bright right above your head. The word Relax is now reverberating through your being. It is there everywhere in your body. Each body cell has been covered by its sheen. Simply hear it and feel it moving through your body.

Practice deep breathing. Take slow, deep and intense breaths to move to the next level. You are completely relaxed now, and are now fully within the mind. There is absolutely no sound from the external world. The physical body is well-protected in its current restful position.

You are in a gently relaxed yet alert position. A powerful and formidable calm is now a part of your being. Breathe out and go past number 8, witnessing it just above your head. The word Relax is now fully immersed into you. It is being gently repeated and communicated to the subconscious.

Take another deep breath. Move into a deeper level of the mind. Relax gently. Breathe out and go past number 9. Do not do anything more. Stay calm. Do not react or make anything. Each thing is being passively created with absolute ease and clarity.

Breathe in slowly, gently and deeply, moving into the deepest consciousness levels that you"ve witnessed. You are filled with relaxation, healing power and energy, which can be monitored.

Feel it in motion. It is taking away all your problems. Witness your body being healed. You are feeling instantly younger. There is a feeling of being renewed, balanced and alive. When you breathe out, the numerical 10 is right over your head. You have completely arrived. There is a deep sense of arrival within your personal space of rejuvenation, relaxation and power. It is time to reveal your glorious, true self.

The door to your personal space is filled with power. It can be anything you want it to be. It takes shape inside your mind. Borrow from childhood memories, when you were completely at ease. There was control, innocence and vision. Now, you get to mould that vision. Look out into the world. Watch natural wonders such as the mountains and beaches take shape right before you.

As you get ready to move into your powerful personal space, the door is slowly sliding back. It exposes a slight trace of sunlight, while beginning to move away. Imagine a stunningly breathtaking landscape. A tranquil river is flowing under the elevator. It slowly trickles and transverses rocky river beds. It travels into a spectacular landscape of lush and nourishing trees. Step out gently.

Feel the cool, soothing water on your naked feet. The rocks feel smooth, serene and grounded. They are firm. There''s no way for you to slip.

You are completely at peace within your personal space of power. There is no care in the world. You can be whatever you fancy. For some time, feel the water licking your feet. It is constantly moving, carrying your thoughts along. Walk through the lush grass and experience its serenity on your toes and feet pads. You are now relaxing under the shade of a large tree. There is a large clearing that is a perfect setting to relax under the scintillating light of the sun. The sun''s rays can be seen cutting through the trees'' branches. The sun''s soothing and gentle rays warmly caress your skin. Clouds are

passing by leisurely, offering you a cool respite. Stay here for a few seconds. Experience a sense of communion with nature. Stop thinking or worrying about the external world.

Your mental state is now restored. It gets this profound feeling that it is where it belongs. It belongs to you. The mind is now one with the body. Carry this sense of oneness all through the day. The powerful personal space is available when it is needed. It can be when you need it the most. Nothing has the ability to cause you harm when you reside in this powerful personal space. No one can enter your personal space

Powerful when you don"t want to let them in. You can get back whenever you want. You are now ready to take care of your loved ones.

Now gently move away from the river, and move to the elevator.
It attempts to take you back to your individual pace. Gradually, each breath draws into a sense of waking awareness. The elevator door slides behind. You are now embarking this journey at the bottommost level. You can spot a pure, white energy surrounding you. The energy, serenity and tranquility are intact.

The energy starts buzzing and surrounds you. You are now able to clearly see the numerical 10 light up over your head. Inhale deeply. Exhale while inching closer to awareness or consciousness. Now, gradually the numerical 9 appears above the head. You feel a greater sense of alertness. You are completely awake now. As you breathe out, you are inching more and more towards waking consciousness and awareness.

You can now slowly spot the numerical 8 just over the head. It has a faint blue inscribed under it. The word is "awake" is written right under the number 8. As you breathe out, you pass the words, going even further. Now you see number 7, and the word, "alert" shining brightly. The soothing blue light emitted by the words brings you greater awareness and focus. Breathe out and slowly move towards a sense of waking awareness.

As you breathe in, spot number 6 right over your head with the words, "awake" written below it. The green light energy around you is gradually turning into a soothing blue. It energizes your mind, body and spirit. Feel it relaxing you and getting the mind into absolute focus.

Breathe in intensely. Draw in the cool blue energy into your belly. The energy is now moving throughout the body. The numerical 5 is now prominently visible over the head. The word, "awake" is getting larger gradually. It is more prominent and defined. It is being repeated in the mind. Feel the vibrations buzzing around throughout your being. Breathe out and feel a sense of transporting into a higher sense of stillness, passing the number.

Breathe completely into the belly, throwing more soothing blue energy into your body. The energy is passing through the head right now. You are completely soaked into its relaxing, serene and soothing effects. The number 4 is now visible over your head, with the word "awake" written under it. It draws you into a greater sense of alertness and

focus reverberating through your body. Now breathe out. Traverse through the number and words into a fully awakened state.

Breathe into the belly using the regular belly breathing method. Soak the soothing blue energy all through your body. Feel a sense of invigoration and stillness. Number 3 is lighting up above you. See the word "alert" just below it. Begin to feel the emotion of alertness and awareness throughout your body. Let the sensation occupy your mind. Sit peacefully. You have chosen to move into a highly alert and awakened breathing state.

Breathe in now with a highly awakened focus. Gradually and faintly, you are able to spot the numerical 2 under the head. You are now resting in a completely conscious and alert state yet opt for stay in the personal cocoon, absorbing every ounce of energy into the body. The word "awake" is now circulating all through the body. The mind is occupied by it too. You have chosen to let this energy fill up your physical and mental faculties. They are conspicuously defined. You feel a natural sense of elation and energy to hear the vibrations of these words with each cell of your body. If infuses you with a sense of joy, calmness, relaxation and positivity. Exhale slowly now into a state of waking consciousness. Carry serenity, energy and relaxation within your senses.

When you inhale, the energy is brought under full control. It brings a sense of mental clarity and energized actions. You are now very slow to witnessing numerical 1, with the term "awake", which has totally engulfed you now. It is deep inside you. Slowly open your eyes. Breathe out. All your worries, stress, tension and anxieties have evaporated. Your mind is completely focused and you are now in absolute control and in a heightened state of being. The energy that has been carried along with you is circulating with the body, bringing you an incomparable sense of calmness and focus all through the day. Recall for a single moment, the jubilation and extreme happiness that has claimed your personal powerful space.

Utilize this blissful feeling to remind yourself all through the day that no one other than you is in control of your life and actions. The feeling will quickly dawn upon you during challenging times. It is a vital part of your being now. The feeling is your second skin. The feeling cannot be forgotten or castaway. It has become a vital component of you.

You are now feeling absolutely relaxed, blissful, focused and prepared to take on the world. Take a moment to lie still and enjoy this blissful feeling. Know that you can draw from it whenever required. Lastly, do not forget to keep a smiling face throughout the day. Enjoy yourself. Enjoy a pleasant, invigorating and refreshing day.

CONCLUSION

Thank you for downloading this amazing book.

I sincerely hope it was successful in helping you fulfill your goal of achieving happiness, positivity and relaxation through meditation.

The next step is to practice the various meditation techniques mentioned in the book, for simply reading about these techniques without applying them is sheer wasted opportunity. The various meditation sessions are packed with clear and simple instructions to get you started with your practice right away. So, do not hesitate to begin using these methods to slip into a dedicated and consistent meditation practice.

Lastly, if you truly enjoyed the book, please take time out to share your thoughts and post a review on Amazon. It"d be highly appreciated!

www.ingramcontent.com/pod-product-compliance
Lightning Source LLC
Chambersburg PA
CBHW071425070526
44578CB00001B/11